Promising Practices for Engaging Families in STEM Learning

A Volume in
Family School Community Partnership Issues

Series Editors

Diana Hiatt-Michael
Pepperdine University
Michael P. Evans
Miami University
Holly Kreider
The Heising-Simons Foundation

Family School Community Partnership Issues

Diana Hiatt-Michael, Michael P. Evans, and Holly Kreider, Editors

Promising Practices for Engaging Families in STEM Learning

edited by

Margaret Caspe
Global Family Research Project

Taniesha A. Woods
Independent Consultant

Joy Lorenzo Kennedy
Databrary

INFORMATION AGE PUBLISHING, INC.
Charlotte, NC • www.infoagepub.com

Library of Congress Cataloging-in-Publication Data

CIP record for this book is available from the Library of Congress
http://www.loc.gov

ISBNs: 978-1-64113-280-0 (Paperback)

978-1-64113-281-7 (Hardcover)

978-1-64113-282-4 (ebook)

CONTENTS

SECTION II: MODELS AND APPROACHES TO ENGAGING FAMILIES IN STEM

SECTION III: POLICIES SUPPORTING FAMILY ENGAGEMENT IN STEM

ACKNOWLEDGMENTS

We would like to thank the authors who contributed to this volume as well as the external reviewers who provided essential insights and feedback: Beth Casey, Marta Civil, Teresa Dunleavy, Rebecca Gomez, Mary Hynes-Berry, Marilou Hyson, Alissa Lange, Keliann LaConte, Maria Zavala, and Jennifer Zosh. Special thanks to Holly Kreider, Diana Hiatt-Michael, and Michael Evans for their leadership in this series.

INTRODUCTION

As this monograph was nearing its final state, we in the continental U.S. were treated to a rare event—a solar eclipse. The eclipse was at once awe-inspiring, beautiful, and an amazing teaching and learning moment for the youngest of children through the oldest of adults. We found ourselves asking questions about the sun and the moon, measuring shadows, puzzling over humanity's part in the universe, and building contraptions like pinhole viewers to watch the astronomical event.

This is the power of STEM—science, technology, engineering, and mathematics. It is lively, exciting, and constantly evolving. STEM education is more than just bringing together four discreet disciplines—it is fundamentally about reimagining how and where we learn, through inquiry, experimentation, and discovery across both school and nonschool settings.

STEM is also a powerful mechanism to connect, engage, and empower families in children's education. STEM provides opportunities for parents and children to spend time together asking fun and meaningful questions that link in-and out-of-school learning. STEM creates new experiences for families to coconstruct and support learning with their children from the earliest years throughout formal schooling and onto college and career pathways. STEM also presents possibilities for families to build confidence and agency in supporting children's interests; especially those families who might be marginalized because of their economic or language status, race, or culture.

For all of these reasons, the goal of this monograph is to explore family engagement in STEM learning. *What do we mean by family engagement?*

Children learn both skills and attitudes from those around them, certainly their mothers and fathers, but also other adult caregivers, like grandparents, aunts, uncles, and babysitters, as well as older siblings. And how families support and guide their children's learning is influenced, in part, by the relationships that families form with school and community educators. So, rather than a unidimensional measure of involvement, like attendance at a PTA meeting, by family engagement we refer to a meaningful two-way dialogue between families and educators. From this perspective, the authors in this monograph highlight how *all* family voices are foundational, informed, and essential ingredients of teaching children the STEM skills they need to be successful in school and throughout life.

We also recognize that just as STEM happens anywhere—in homes, schools, parks, and libraries—so too does family engagement take place in all settings in which children learn. For this reason, the authors in this monograph focus their research in settings that include early childhood programs, schools, museums, and other community institutions. Last, while the focus of this monograph is primarily on family engagement in the early and elementary school years, we appreciate that engagement persists throughout the middle and high school years, and beyond. Many of the authors position their early family engagement and STEM work as a stepping stone for building strong, lasting family engagement trajectories.

And one caveat. Although we understand and appreciate that STEM is a multidimensional and integrated concept, we also acknowledge that, in many cases, the research throughout this monograph attends to only parts of the STEM equation (e.g., a focus on math anxiety or science conversations). In part, this is a result of researchers' interests and their intentionally striving to tease apart the mechanisms for how family engagement in STEM learning exerts its influence on children. It is also a result of the limitations in measurement we have for assessing children's learning. Mindful of this challenge, throughout the monograph we have tried to achieve balance in the four domains.

—Margaret Caspe, Taniesha A. Woods, and Joy Lorenzo Kennedy

SECTION I

THEORIES AND FRAMEWORKS FOR UNDERSTANDING FAMILY ENGAGEMENT IN STEM

In Section I of the monograph, we provide theoretical and research paradigms and practical examples and strategies to enhance family engagement in STEM. Our hope is to set the stage for the volume by laying out a strong evidence and research-base for the importance of families' engagement in STEM learning. In the first chapter, Caspe and Lopez describe five key processes that school and community educators can use to engage families in STEM. These include *reaching out* to families and *raising up* their voices, in order to make families more aware of the opportunities that already exist for STEM learning in children's lives; *reinforcing* the STEM learning opportunities in the community and home environments in order to help parents gain the knowledge, skills, and confidence they need to promote their children's STEM learning; building *relationships* with families around STEM learning to encourage children to stay motivated and take risks; and *reimagining* partnerships among parents, schools, and community institutions like museums and libraries where STEM learning occurs.

However, children face a host of challenges to STEM learning—from the transmission of adults' anxiety and lack of confidence in their own STEM skills, to inequalities in out-of-school learning opportunities, to biases and misconceptions about the kinds of STEM supports offered by families from low-income and immigrant homes. In the second chapter, Berkowitz, Schaeffer, Rozek, Beilock, and Levine address how parents' math anxiety—fear and apprehension of doing mathematics—can lead to intergenerational effects on mathematical learning and attitudes of children. They then provide suggestions for how math anxious parents can best support their children's mathematical learning through mathematics storybooks and apps and participation in interventions that help families feel comfortable using math talk in their everyday lives.

In the third chapter, Solis and Callanan explore how deficit assumptions about cultural difference can have negative implications for Latino children in science classrooms. Using conversational data from two studies of Mexican-heritage children and families, the authors show that common deficit assumptions are incorrect. Solis and Callanan argue that by making families' strengths, skills, and ideas visible to educators, we can more effectively engage families in STEM learning.

In the final chapter of this section, Brown, Schreiber, and Barbarin underscore the unique challenges that African American children face in mathematics education due to issues of discrimination, and highlight the role of family engagement as a source of resilience that supports children and sets them on pathways to academic success. The chapter reviews promising practices and provides recommendations about how school leaders, teachers, and families can work together to positively influence mathematical outcomes for African American children.

Together these chapters show that by working together and recognizing each other's strengths and expertise, educators and families can develop meaningful opportunities for family STEM learning that motivate children and help them develop the skills they need to be successful in school and beyond.

CHAPTER 1

THE 5Rs

Research-Based Strategies for Engaging Families in STEM Learning

Margaret Caspe and M. Elena Lopez

When Luna and her 10-year-old daughter Maya signed up for the Make-HER workshop at the Sunnyvale Public Library they were both excited and also a little anxious; they were eager to spend time together but neither felt particularly comfortable in their math and science skills. The workshop began with the facilitator posing a challenge to the mother-daughter teams: build a lantern that can light up using only the sound of your breath. The facilitator provided the teams with a variety of materials including conductive copper tape, batteries, a microprocessor and microphone, a gumdrop LED, and a circuit template. Feeling a little overwhelmed, Maya and Luna got right to work. They gave each other a high five and started to laugh when they got their lantern to light, but making the light responsive to sound coming through the microphone was a bit more challenging. Maya and Luna persevered—and with some help of the facilitator and another mother-daughter team—they did it. As they left the library that night, Maya and Luna felt more connected, and saw STEM in a way they never had before.[1]

Science, technology, engineering, and mathematics (STEM) is not just about what students learn in the confines of their classrooms, but can also be a family affair. Over 50 years of research from fields including neuroscience, developmental psychology, and education confirm that when families are engaged in learning, children are more likely to succeed both

---

Promising Practices for Engaging Families in STEM Learning, pp. 3–17
Copyright © 2018 by Information Age Publishing

academically and socially in school and beyond (Jeynes, 2012; Van Voorhis, Maier, Epstein, & Lloyd, 2013). Research also shows that family engagement efforts are most effective when they are systemic. This means that schools and communities go beyond random isolated acts of engaging families, and instead weave family engagement practices throughout an entire program and across learning settings—such as homes, afterschool programs, museums, and libraries (Weiss, Lopez, & Rosenberg, 2010). The purpose of this chapter is to provide a set of research-based processes that can guide educators in schools and informal learning settings to move family engagement in STEM from the periphery to the center. When implemented comprehensively, these processes are likely to pull families into STEM activities and to sustain their continued encouragement of their children's interest in science, technology, engineering and mathematics.

FAMILY ENGAGEMENT AND STEM

Family engagement is a shared responsibility among families, schools, and communities to support children's learning. It is not a one-size-fits-all program or approach—but rather it is about building relationships and trust between families, schools, and communities to enable families to advocate for and promote children's learning. It encompasses the ways that schools and communities open doors so that families have the knowledge, skills, and confidence to advance their children's learning effectively. Moreover, family engagement is most powerful when it takes place across children's development, from birth through young adulthood (Englund, Egeland, & Collins, 2008; Hayakawa, Englund, Warner-Richter, & Reynolds, 2013; Weiss et al., 2010).

The importance of family engagement follows from a theoretical understanding of the ecological nature of human development (Bronfenbrenner, 1979). This school of thought takes into account the complex set of influences on learning and development originating from a person's experiences across multiple and interconnected settings (e.g., home, school, playground, libraries, media, etc.). For this reason, family engagement is not just about the ways that families support education in schools, but rather, it is the ways that families support learning anywhere, anytime. Family learning experiences can range from everyday activities and routines families have (e.g., visiting the supermarket, relaxing at home), to involvement in designed environments like libraries, museums, and science centers, and to participation in more structured family engagement programs in schools, out-of-school time, and summer programs (Bell, Lewenstein, Shouse, & Feder, 2009; Ridge, Weisberg, Ilgaz, Hirsh-Pasek, & Golinkoff, 2014).

A number of definitional attributes of STEM make family engagement not an "add-on" but an essential feature:

- **STEM is more than just an acronym**. It is about how science, technology, engineering, and mathematics are fundamentally interconnected and how knowledge in one subject supports and complements knowledge in another. Yet, STEM instruction in school is frequently limited. Although many professional standards have begun to call for the teaching of STEM in an integrated, hands-on and interdisciplinary manner (Next Generation Science Standards, 2013; U.S. Department of Education & Office of Innovation and Improvement, 2016), opportunities to understand the interconnected relevance of STEM in everyday life are often best achieved through family and community approaches. For example, project-based activities—whether putting together a jigsaw puzzle or stacking a tower of blocks—are opportunities for families to build conversations about the various components of STEM. Furthermore, formal STEM projects can facilitate deep conversations not just between adults and children, but also among teen mentors, parents, and children in Maker Spaces, libraries, and museums.
- **STEM learning starts early, before children enter formal education.** Very young children are much more capable of learning STEM concepts and practices than originally thought, with a growing number of studies showing a correlation between early experiences with STEM and later success, making family engagement in STEM in the earliest years and throughout the school years critical (Watts, Duncan, Siegler, & Davis-Kean, 2014).
- **STEM is culturally imbued.** STEM is not a set of disciplines about formulas and algorithms that exist in the vacuum of a lab or a classroom. Instead, STEM education involves interactions among children and adults, both in schools and in the community, based in part on their values, beliefs, and culture (Civil, 2016).
- **STEM learning takes place everywhere.** Those who are successful at STEM tinker with ideas and think about it all the time. STEM learning and experiences today are not confined to schools. Families appreciate the opportunity for out-of-school STEM activities in which they can actively relate with their children in questioning, learning, and discovery (Randi Korn & Associates, 2011).

Although the importance of family engagement is confirmed by research, how to effectively engage families in STEM learning is not well-examined. This is unfortunate because in today's world, students need to be equipped with new core knowledge and skills: to problem solve, be curious, gather and evaluate evidence, and make sense of the large volume of information they receive from varied print and digital media—all skills which family engagement in STEM learning can provide (U.S. Department of Education & Office of Innovation and Improvement, 2016).

Family engagement in STEM is also a matter of equity. STEM has historically served as a gateway for students to enter higher education and higher-paid occupations. Unless STEM education is equally accessible to underserved children and families, the social and economic inequalities that exist in education and our society are likely to continue. Moreover, family engagement matters most, and exerts its greatest impact, on those students who are most vulnerable, particularly by virtue of their socioeconomic status (Dearing, Kreider, Simpkins, & Weiss, 2006; Schulting, Malone, & Dodge, 2005). For this reason, STEM initiatives that integrate family engagement have added value in their potential to reduce opportunity gaps.

THE 5Rs: PROCESSES TO PROMOTE FAMILY ENGAGEMENT IN STEM LEARNING

The remainder of this chapter explores a set of connected processes to build family engagement in STEM across the many contexts in which children and youth learn. The processes reflect the findings of research on family engagement in diverse settings such as schools, early childhood programs, and libraries. The five family engagement processes—*reach out, raise up, reinforce, relate,* and *reimagine*—when coupled with strong leadership and resources, have the potential to provide families with the knowledge, guidance, and inspiration to support their children's STEM development from the early years all the way through high school (Lopez, Caspe, & McWilliams, 2016; Weiss, Caspe, Lopez, & McWilliams, 2016). Our hope is that STEM educators will reflect on these processes in their current and future work. We use the term "STEM educators" broadly to refer to early childhood educators and teachers in school settings, community educators like librarians and afterschool staff who actively promote STEM through programming, as well as front-line staff in museums and science centers who might promote STEM through everyday interactions with families in their spaces.

Reach Out: STEM Educators Actively Seek to Make Contact With Families, and Take Steps to Be Inclusive

Research shows that welcoming institutions and teacher invitations for families to participate motivate families to get involved (Hoover-Dempsey et al., 2005; see also Duch & Genetian, this volume, Chapter 5). In schools, reaching out might exist on a continuum ranging from teachers communicating with parents about standards, curriculum, and children's STEM progress, to creating mobile STEM classrooms that travel to different sections of a community. Family STEM nights are an especially popular way for schools to reach out to families, give them opportunities to learn about what engineers do, learn about children's interests and abilities in STEM, and come to see STEM as an enjoyable and fun experience (MacDonald & Mauer, 2015; Smetana, Schumaker, Goldfien, & Nelson, 2012; Yanowitz & Hahs-Vaughn, 2016).

In informal learning settings, like afterschool programs, reaching out involves making sure that families have access to existing opportunities, know how to enroll their children, and have information about what students will learn in the program. For example, Sparklelab (www.sparklelab. ph) in the Philippines pays attention to messaging. It invites parents and children to try out free workshops where together they can "make learning extraordinary." It uses popular communication methods such as social media, e-mail, text messaging, the press, community fairs and partnerships, and importantly, word of mouth among participating adults and children. Sparklelab uses language that debunks myths that both families and children may have about STEM, such as girls not liking or being good at mathematics and science, or that science and mathematics are boring and only for geeks.

Designed environments like museums, libraries, and nature centers—which can sometimes be intimidating and disorienting for families who are not accustomed to them (Archer, Dawson, Seakins, & Wong, 2016)—often rely on their physical environments and front-line staff to make families aware of learning opportunities. For example, when museums post signs providing information about the specific ways in which an exhibit might provide learning opportunities in language, science, or mathematics, parents give exhibits higher academic ratings and are similar to experts in their assessments of learning opportunities within them (Song et al., 2017). These settings thus can increase family engagement by ensuring information is displayed in clear and simple language and positioned in visible spaces where parents will see it (Nadelson, 2013). Front-line staff and volunteers can also use a variety of strategies to introduce themselves to families and define their role as a potential learning facilitator, including greeting visitors, inviting them to participate in an activity, asking check-in questions, offering guidance or tips, or simply inserting themselves into a conversation or interaction (Pattison & Dierking, 2012).

Raise Up: STEM Educators Elevate Family Perspectives to Develop and Improve Programs and Services

Families have important knowledge, feedback, and input for programs and by asking for, listening to, and responding to family members' views—

both formally and informally—STEM educators can empower families and improve STEM services. Raising up a family's voice is also a mechanism to ensure that STEM programs are culturally responsive and relevant to a learner's community and cultural orientation (Kayumova, Karsli, Allexsaht-Snider, & Buxton, 2015).

The funds of knowledge approach is one method to raise up family voices in STEM learning (González, Moll, & Amanti, 2005). The funds of knowledge approach focuses on culturally-situated everyday practices that take place in homes and communities. Instead of replicating and transmitting school values and activities to the home, this approach reframes family-school relationships by putting families' knowledge and experiences at the heart of both the classroom and parenting programs. Research by Marta Civil and colleagues shows that educators can create meaningful mathematical and STEM family learning experiences by finding families' everyday mathematical practices through household ethnographic interviews and observations, and then developing mathematical workshops that build from the math concepts already embedded in household activities (Civil, 2016; Díez-Palomar, Menéndez, & Civil, 2011; Menéndez & Civil, 2008). For example, families might explore the mathematics embedded in sewing or tiling floors—a research project based on lived experiences (see Chapter 6 this volume). Although conducting in depth research projects is often not feasible—or desirable—for schools and other STEM programs, partnering with universities can support this work. University-practice partnerships can open up new understandings of STEM in families' everyday lives, and they can also benefit universities by creating spaces for preservice teachers to come to understand families' strengths and opportunities better (Bottoms, Ciechanowski, Jones, de la Hoz, & Fonseca, 2017) (see Figure 1.1).

Reinforce: STEM Educators Guide and Model the Specific Actions That Families Can Take to Support STEM Learning

Research points to three main ways that families strengthen STEM learning: (1) a STEM-rich home environment, (2) a mindset that promotes strong STEM identities, and (3) participation in supportive STEM interactions with their children. STEM educators have a role in guiding and supporting each.

Reinforcing the home environment is particularly important in the early years. Research shows that building with blocks, geometric toys and shape sorters, playing puzzles, reading books with mathematical content, counting objects and playing counting games are linked to children's early mathematical skills (Goldstein, Cole, & Cordes, 2016; Gunderson &

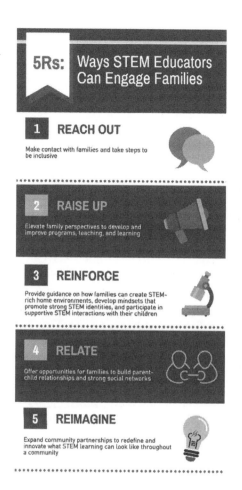

Figure 1.1. Ways STEM educators can engage families.

Levine, 2011; Verdine et al., 2014; Zosh et al., 2015). And these findings persist across different cultural groups. Having more children's books at home (even without mathematical content), and parents who frequently practice numbers with children (e.g., reading, writing, or working with numbers, such as reading a calendar or working on homework), are both independently associated with *higher* math achievement for Latino children starting kindergarten (Murphey, Madill, & Guzman, 2017).

Reinforcing mindsets recognizes family influences on children's STEM confidence, expectations for success, and career aspirations—particularly from early adolescence through young adulthood. Perceived family support for STEM learning is associated with children's interest in science and feelings of self-efficacy, which in turn influences their choices for and engagement in science learning (Sha, Schunn, Bathgate, & Ben-Eliyahu, 2016). Growth and changes in youth's mathematical achievement from 7th through 12th grade are influenced by parents' intrinsic motivational practices and efforts to promote persistence in STEM careers (Ing, 2014). When reflecting on their K–12 education, high achieving African American college students majoring in STEM count their parents' beliefs in their abilities to complete tasks and reach goals as one of the major contributors to their success (McGee & Spencer, 2015). STEM educators can share with families how simply holding high expectations and positive beliefs can strongly influence their children's STEM development—especially when this support helps parents overcome any gender-related stereotypes about mathematics that parents may have (Denner, Laursen, Dickson, & Hart, 2016).

STEM educators can also reinforce families' participation in supportive STEM interactions with their children. When parents have elaborate conversations with their children at home (e.g., asking open-ended memory questions and using descriptive language), school age children talk more with their families about science lessons of which parents have no prior specific knowledge than school age children whose parents used more close-ended prompts (Leichtman et al., 2017). Adolescent girls have stronger spatial skills when mothers embed high quality assistance and cognitive stimulation within conversations and teaching tasks (Casey, Dearing, Dulaney, Heyman, & Springer, 2014). These techniques include mothers communicating task objectives; providing appropriate feedback that matches child focus, is reasonably paced, and is presented in clear and logical steps; and prompting the child with questions to stimulate thinking and problem solving.

STEM educators can reinforce conversational techniques by sending home activity packets, providing workshops and family science nights, and even offering brief educational sessions (Hynes-Berry & Berry, 2014; Reinhart et al., 2016; Thomas, Raisor, & Goebel, 2013). For instance, a modest educational program in which a museum staff member gave parents engineering tips about building structures, as well as instructions about how to converse with their children, changed parent-child interactions. Parents doubled the number of Why-questions they asked their children and produced more STEM-related talk during building than those parents who did not receive the brief intervention (Haden et al., 2014). As a different example, Family Creative Learning is a series of workshops that educators in various settings can implement to engage children and families together in creating their own projects using the Scratch programming language and Makey Makey invention kit. From the workshops, families learn mathematical and computational ideas and practices, perspectives about themselves and the increasingly digital and networked world around them, and how to learn in playful and exploratory ways (Roque & Leggett, 2017).

Relate: STEM Educators Offer Opportunities for Families and Children to Learn Together and Build Parent-Child Relationships

When learning interactions occur within the context of positive parent-child relationships, children are more likely to enjoy the activities, stay motivated, take risks, and persevere with difficult problems (Dweck, 2007; Gonzalez-DeHass, Willems, & Holbein, 2005). Family science nights, museums trips, and STEM-focused programming as described in the opening vignette to this chapter, are all opportunities for families to bond, form relationships, and spend fun, engaging, and special time together while learning STEM concepts (Archer et al., 2016). For example, in one study of family learning in a science museum in Mexico, families reflected that the museum served as a context for relaxed family interactions, funny anecdotes, and occasions to learn to communicate and learn new aspects of family dynamics. Moreover, exhibits that provide opportunities for families to learn science and tell stories about relevant history—for example, an investigation of the science behind earthquakes and the destruction they can cause—can be particularly memorable and emotional (Briseño-Garzón, 2013).

STEM educators also offer opportunities for families to build peer-to-peer relationships and increase social networks. Through connections to other families made in libraries, museums, or other STEM-related programs or settings, families can expand their support networks, reduce isolation, and gain access to community resources. STEM educators can do this by taking time during workshops or other events for parents to meet, talk and get to know one another. They can also gather families for casual events where children and different families play games together with a science focus. Having varied social networks promotes family well-being, especially among families living in poverty, and is linked to families feeling more self-confident and better able to provide home environments with greater cognitive stimulation (Marshall, Noonan, McCartney, Marx, & Keefe, 2001; Small, 2009).

Reimagine: STEM Educators Collaborate With Multiple Partners to Redefine and Innovate What STEM Learning Can Look Like Throughout a Community

Community cooperation and collaboration allow organizations to share and align mechanisms for outreach, recruitment, space, funding, staff, and curriculum. These partnerships can be critical in filling specific learning gaps during afterschool hours or the summer months, particularly important for children living in poverty. Partnerships also enable planning and creating more equitable pathways for family engagement and children's achievement. For example, the Science-Technology Activities and Resources Library Education Network (STAR_Net), is a partnership among the American Library Association, the Lunar and Planetary Institute, and the Afterschool Alliance that transforms libraries into museum-like hands-on interplanetary exhibits. The initiative provides training and resources to library staff so librarians can support STEM learning in free spaces, like the library, for parents for whom the cost and logistics of getting to a museum are too exorbitant (Fitzhugh & Coulon, 2015).

Two additional community partners that can support reimagined STEM learning pathways are universities and private philanthropies. For example, partnerships with universities can make evaluation and integration of cutting edge-science into curriculum possible. Foundations can also play a critical role by providing funds to explore partnerships and seed innovation. For example, to support the development of early math skills while leveraging families' power to engage children in the learning process, the Heising-Simons Foundation awarded grants to five diverse family engagement programs—ranging from early childhood and community-based programs to pediatrician's offices—to develop, test, and integrate early mathematics learning into their usual activities (Harris, Petersen, & Wulsin, 2017).

CONCLUSION

In this chapter, we have shown how a research-based set of family engagement processes can open the door for innovative ways to embed family engagement into STEM initiatives. By *reaching out* to families and *raising up* their voices, STEM educators raise awareness among families of the opportunities that exist for STEM learning in school and in the community, and are better able to develop programs that are culturally relevant to learners. By *reinforcing* the STEM home environment, parents' STEM mindsets, and parents' roles related to STEM, STEM educators are able to give parents the knowledge, skills, and confidence they need to promote their children's STEM learning. Even more, when STEM educators help students learn STEM, as well as build *relationships* with their families around it, children are more likely to stay motivated and take risks. Finally, we have also highlighted how, by *reimagining* partnerships among myriad institutions where STEM learning occurs, STEM educators are creating multiple pathways by which families can get involved in their children's learning over time and across settings. Our hope is that the identification of these five processes proves useful in considering chapters across this book as well as in future work and initiatives.

NOTE

1. This vignette is a compilation of perspectives developed from interviews and vignettes from the MakHer website blog (2016). Lantern luminaries. https://sunnyvalemakeher.wordpress.com/2016/11/08/november-1-2016-lantern-luminaries/

REFERENCES

Archer, L., Dawson, E., Seakins, A., & Wong, B. (2016). Disorientating, fun or meaningful? Disadvantaged families' experiences of a science museum visit. *Cultural Studies of Science Education*, *11*, 917–939. https://doi.org/10.1007/s11422-015-9667-7

Bell, P., Lewenstein, B., Shouse, A. W., & Feder, M. A. (Eds.). (2009). *Learning science in informal environments: People, places, and pursuits*. Washington, DC: National Academies Press.

Bottoms, S. I., Ciechanowski, K., Jones, K., de la Hoz, J., & Fonseca, A. L. (2017). Leveraging the community context of Family Math and Science Nights to develop culturally responsive teaching practices. *Teaching and Teacher Education*, *61*, 1–15. https://doi.org/10.1016/j.tate.2016.09.006

Briseño-Garzón, A. (2013). More than science: Family learning in a Mexican science museum. *Cultural Studies of Science Education*, *8*, 307–327. https://doi.org/10.1007/s11422-012-9477-0

Bronfenbrenner, U. (1979). *The ecology of human development: Experiments by nature design*. Cambridge, MA: Harvard University Press.

Casey, B. M., Dearing, E., Dulaney, A., Heyman, M., & Springer, R. (2014). Young girls' spatial and arithmetic performance: The mediating role of maternal supportive interactions during joint spatial problem solving. *Early Childhood Research Quarterly*, *29*, 636–648. https://doi.org/10.1016/j.ecresq.2014.07.005

Civil, M. (2016). STEM learning research through a funds of knowledge lens. *Cultural Studies of Science Education*, *11*, 41–59. https://doi.org/10.1007/s11422-014-9648-2

Dearing, E., Kreider, H., Simpkins, S., & Weiss, H. B. (2006). Family involvement in school and low-income children's literacy performance: Longitudinal associations between and within families. *Journal of Educational Psychology*, *98*, 653–664. https://doi.org/10.1037/0022-0663.98.4.653

Denner, J., Laursen, B., Dickson, D., & Hart, A. C. (2016). Latino children's math confidence: The role of mothers' gender stereotypes and involvement across the transition to middle school. *Journal of Early Adolescence*, 1–17. https://doi.org/10.1177/0272431616675972

Díez-Palomar, J., Menéndez, J. M., & Civil, M. (2011). Learning mathematics with adult learners: Drawing from parents' perspective. *Revista Latinoamericana de Investigación en Matemática Educativa*, *14*, 71–94.

Dweck, C. (2007). *Mindset: The new psychology of success*. New York, NY: Ballantine.

Englund, M. M., Egeland, B., & Collins, W. A. (2008). Exceptions to high school dropout predictions in a low-income sample: Do adults make a difference? *Journal of Social Issues*, *64*(1), 77–94. https://doi.org/10.1111/j.1540-4560.2008.00549.x

Fitzhugh, G., & Coulon, V. (2015, August). *Can libraries provide STEM learning experiences for patrons? Findings from the Star_Net project summative evaluation*. Paper presented at the Public Libraries & STEM Conference, Denver, Colorado. Retrieved from http://www.nc4il.org/images/stem-in-libraries/evaluation/Can-Libraries-Provide-STEM-Learning-Experiences.pdf

Goldstein, A., Cole, T., & Cordes, S. (2016). How parents read counting books and non-numerical books to their preverbal infants: An observational study. *Frontiers in Psychology*, *7*, 1–10. https://doi.org/10.3389/fpsyg.2016.01100

González, N., Moll, L., & Amanti, C. (2005). *Funds of knowledge: Theorizing practices in households, communities, and classrooms*. Mahwah, New Jersey: Lawrence Erlbaum Associates.

Gonzalez-DeHass, A. R., Willems, P. P., & Holbein, M. F. D. (2005). Examining the relationship between parental involvement and student motivation. *Educational Psychology Review*, *17*, 99–123. https://doi.org/10.1007/s10648-005-3949-7

Gunderson, E. A., & Levine, S. C. (2011). Some types of parent number talk count more than others: Relations between parents' input and children's cardinal-number knowledge. *Developmental Science*, *14*, 1021–1032. https://doi.org/10.1111/j.1467-7687.2011.01050.x

Haden, C. A., Jant, E. A., Hoffman, P. C., Marcus, M., Geddes, J. R., & Gaskins, S. (2014). Supporting family conversations and children's STEM learning in a children's museum. *Early Childhood Research Quarterly*, *29*, 333–344. https://doi.org/10.1016/j.ecresq.2014.04.004

Harris, B., Petersen, D., & Wulsin, C. S. (2017). *Integrating mathematical thinking into family engagement programs*. Princeton, NJ: Mathematica Policy Research. Retrieved from https://www.mathematica-mpr.com/our-publications-and-findings/publications/integrating-mathematical-thinking-into-family-engagement-programs

Hayakawa, M., Englund, M. M., Warner-Richter, M., & Reynolds, A. J. (2013). Early parent involvement and school achievement: A longitudinal path analysis. *NHSA Dialog: The Research-to-Practice Journal for the Early Childhood Field*, *16*(1), 200–204. Retrieved from https://journals.uncc.edu/dialog/index

Hoover-Dempsey, K. V., Walker, J. M. T., Sandler, H. M., Whetsel, D., Green, C. L., Wilkins, A. S., & Closson, K. (2005). Why do parents become involved? Research findings and implications. *Elementary School Journal*, *106*, 105–130. https://doi.org/10.1086/499194

Hynes-Berry, M., & Berry, G. (2014). "Reading an object": Developing effective scientific inquiry using student questions. *European Journal of Science and Mathematics Education*, *2*, 87–97. Retrieved from http://scimath.net/

Ing, M. (2014). Can parents influence children's mathematics achievement and persistence in STEM careers? *Journal of Career Development*, *41*, 87–103. https://doi.org/10.1177/0894845313481672

Jeynes, W. (2012). A meta-analysis of the efficacy of different types of parental involvement programs for urban students. *Urban Education*, *47*, 706–742. https://doi.org/10.1177/0042085912445643

Kayumova, S., Karsli, E., Allexsaht-Snider, M., & Buxton, C. (2015). Latina mothers and daughters: Ways of knowing, being, and becoming in the context of bilingual family science workshops. *Anthropology & Education Quarterly*, *46*, 260–276. https://doi.org/10.1111/aeq.12106

Leichtman, M. D., Camilleri, K. A., Pillemer, D. B., Amato-Wierda, C. C., Hogan, J. E., & Dongo, M. D. (2017). Talking after school: Parents' conversational styles and children's memory for a science lesson. *Journal of Experimental Child Psychology*, *156*, 1–15. https://doi.org/10.1016/j.jecp.2016.11.002

Lopez, M. E., Caspe, M., & McWilliams, L. (2016). *Public libraries: A vital space for family engagement*. Cambridge, MA: Harvard Family Research Project. Retrieved from https://globalfrp.org/Articles/Libraries-for-the-21st-Century-It-s-A-Family-Thing

MacDonald, S., & Mauer, M. (2015). Families learning together. *Science & Children*, *52*(9), 44–49. Retrieved from http://www.nsta.org/elementaryschool/

Marshall, N. L., Noonan, A. E., McCartney, K., Marx, F., & Keefe, N. (2001). It takes an urban village: Parenting networks of urban families. *Journal of Family Issues*, *22*, 163–182. https://doi.org/10.1177/019251301022002003

McGee, E., & Spencer, M. B. (2015). Black parents as advocates, motivators, and teachers of mathematics. *The Journal of Negro Education*, *84*, 473–490. https://doi.org/10.7709/jnegroeducation.84.3.0473

Menéndez, J. M., & Civil, M. (2008). Mathematics workshops for parents: An example of non-formal adult education. *Adult Learning*, *19*, 17–20. https://doi.org/10.1177/104515950801900304

Murphey, D., Madill, R., & Guzman, L. (2017). *Making math count more for young Latino children*. Washington, DC: Child Trends. Retrieved from https://www.childtrends.org/publications/making-math-count-young-latino-children/

Nadelson, L. S. (2013). Who is watching and who is playing: Parental engagement with children at a hands-on science center. *The Journal of Educational Research*, *106*, 478–484. https://doi.org/10.1080/00220671.2013.833010

Next Generation Science Standards. (2013). *Next generation science standards*. Retrieved from http://www.nextgenscience.org/

Pattison, S. A., & Dierking, L. D. (2012). Exploring staff facilitation that supports family learning. *Journal of Museum Education*, *37*(3), 69–80. https://doi.org/10.1080/10598650.2012.11510743

Randi Korn & Associates, Inc. (2011). *Summative evaluation: Children's library and discovery center at Queens Central Library*. Alexandria, VA. Retrieved from http://www.informalscience.org/sites/default/files/2011_RKA_QueensLibrary_Summative_dist.pdf

Reinhart, M., Bloomquist, D., Strickler-Eppard, L., Czerniak, C. M., Gilbert, A., Kaderavek, J., & Molitor, S. C. (2016). Taking science home: Connecting schools and families through science activity packs for young children. *School Science and Mathematics*, *116*, 3–16. https://doi.org/10.1111/ssm.12152

Ridge, K. E., Weisberg, D. S., Ilgaz, H., Hirsh-Pasek, K. A., & Golnikoff, R. M. (2014). Supermarket speak: Increasing talk among low-socioeconomic status families. *Mind, Brain, and Education*, *9*, 127–135. https://doi.org/10.1111/mbe.12081

Roque, R., & Leggett, S. (2017). *Family creative learning: Facilitator Guide*. Retrieved from http://familycreativelearning.org

Schulting, A. B., Malone, P. S., & Dodge, K. A. (2005). The effect of school-based kindergarten transition policies and practices on child academic outcomes. *Developmental Psychology*, *41*, 860–871. https://doi.org/10.1037/0012-1649.41.6.860

Sha, L., Schunn, C., Bathgate, M., & Ben-Eliyahu, A. (2016). Families support their children's success in science learning by influencing interest and self-efficacy. *Journal of Research in Science Teaching*, *53*, 450–472. https://doi.org/10.1002/tea.21251

Small, M. L. (2009). *Unanticipated gain: Origins of network inequality in everyday life*. New York: Oxford University Press.

Smetana, L. K., Schumaker, J. C., Goldfien, W. S., & Nelson, C. (2012). Family style engineering. *Science & Children*, *50*(4), 67–71. Retrieved from http://www.nsta.org/elementaryschool/

Song, L., Golinkoff, R. M., Stuehling, A., Resnick, I., Mahajan, N., Hirsh-Pasek, K., & Thompson, N. (2017). Parents' and experts' awareness of learning opportunities in children's museum exhibits. *Journal of Applied Developmental Psychology*, *49*, 39–45. https://doi.org/10.1016/j.appdev.2017.01.006

Thomas, J. A., Raisor, J. M., & Goebel, V. (2013). Oh, what Dr. Seuss can induce: Using intentionality to connect families with classrooms through science and children's literature. *Science Activities*, *50*, 31–40. https://doi.org/10.1080/00368121.2012.761172

U.S. Department of Education & Office of Innovation and Improvement. (2016). *STEM 2026: A vision for innovation in STEM education*. Washington, DC. Retrieved from https://innovation.ed.gov/files/2016/09/AIR-STEM2026_Report_2016.pdf

Van Voorhis, F. L., Maier, M. F., Epstein, J. L., & Lloyd, C. M. (2013). *The impact of family involvement on the education of children ages 3 to 8: A focus on literacy and math achievement outcomes and social-emotional skills*. New York, NY: MDRC. Retrieved from http://www.mdrc.org/publication/impact-family-involvement-education-children-ages-3-8

Verdine, B. N., Golinkoff, R. M., Hirsh-Pasek, K., Newcombe, N. S., Filipowicz, A. T., & Chang, A. (2014). Deconstructing building blocks: Preschoolers' spatial assembly performance relates to early mathematical skills. *Child Development*, *85*, 1062–1076. https://doi.org/10.1111/cdev.12165

Watts, T. W., Duncan, G. J., Siegler, R. S., & Davis-Kean, P. E. (2014). What's past is prologue: Relations between early mathematics knowledge and high school achievement. *Educational Researcher*, *43*, 352–360. https://doi.org/10.3102/0013189X14553660

Weiss, H., Caspe, M., Lopez, M. E., & McWilliams, L. (2016). *Ideabook: Libraries for families.* Cambridge, MA: Harvard Family Research Project. Retrieved from https://globalfrp.org/Articles/Libraries-for-the-21st-Century-It-s-A-Family-Thing

Weiss, H. B., Lopez, M. E., & Rosenberg, H. (2010). *Beyond random acts: Family, school, and community engagement as an integral part of education reform.* Cambridge, MA: Harvard Family Research Project.

Yanowitz, K., & Hahs-Vaughn, D. L. (2016). Adults' perceptions of children's science abilities and interest after participating in a family science night. *School Science and Mathematics, 116,* 55–64. https://doi.org/10.1111/ssm.12149

Zosh, J. M., Verdine, B. N., Filipowicz, A., Golinkoff, R. M., Hirsh-Pasek, K., & Newcombe, N. S. (2015). Talking shape: Parental language with electronic versus traditional shape sorters. *Mind, Brain, and Education, 9,* 136–144. https://doi.org/10.1111/mbe.12082

CHAPTER 2

SUPPORTING SCIENCE, TECHNOLOGY, ENGINEERING, AND MATHEMATICS (STEM) LEARNING BY HELPING FAMILIES OVERCOME MATH ANXIETY

Talia Berkowitz, Marjorie W. Schaeffer, Christopher S. Rozek, Sian L. Beilock, and Susan C. Levine

A mother sits down to help her child with homework. As the child pulls out a worksheet covered in numbers, the mother lets out a small groan.

"Not more math homework!" she exclaims. "Math is so hard." The mother takes the worksheet from her child's hands and starts to look over the questions. She talks through how to solve each of the problems as her child sits next to her, listening attentively. As each problem is solved, the child writes in the answer before moving on to the next one. Before they know it, the worksheet is done.

"Phew," says the mom, "I expected that to be a lot worse. I can't wait until you don't have to take any more math classes."

Promising Practices for Engaging Families in STEM Learning, pp. 19–34

The scene described above exemplifies the kinds of mathematics interactions that children of parents with high math anxiety may encounter at home. Small, seemingly mundane exchanges like these can have broad implications for children's mathematical achievement and their likelihood of pursuing science, technology, engineering, and mathematics (STEM) academic and career paths.

As a cornerstone of the STEM domains, a firm grasp of basic mathematical concepts is a crucial component for success in school, the workplace, and everyday life. Although early mathematical skills are a strong predictor of later mathematical achievement, somewhat surprisingly they are also a strong predictor of later reading achievement—even more so than early reading achievement (Duncan et al., 2007). This relationship between early mathematical skills and later academic success across domains may be explained by the higher order thinking skills necessary for success at mathematics, even during the early childhood years. Unfortunately, in the United States, achievement in mathematics is stagnating—students have not shown significant improvements in mathematics in the past 10 years (National Assessment of Educational Progress, 2015), and continue to fall behind their peers in other developed countries, placing 31st among 35 countries on the 2015 PISA test (Organisation for Economic Co-operation and Development, 2016).

Within the United States, differences in mathematical achievement are present early in life. Individual variations in mathematical knowledge emerge prior to kindergarten (Clements & Sarama, 2007; Entwisle & Alexander, 1990; Griffin, Case, & Siegler, 1994; Klibanoff, Levine, Huttenlocher, Vasilyeva, & Hedges, 2006; Starkey, Klein, & Wakeley, 2004) and tend to persist as children progress through school. Children from lower socioeonomic backgrounds are more likely to show early gaps in mathematical knowledge, and these gaps tend to widen over the years (Jordan & Levine, 2009; Levine, Gunderson, & Huttenlocher, 2011; Reardon, 2011). By high school graduation, children from families in the lowest socioeconomic status (SES) decile lag behind their higher income peers by a difference of approximately one standard deviation in mathematical achievement (Reardon, 2011). Addressing the SES-related mathematical achievement gap is closely related to issues of equity given projections of rapid growth in STEM-related job opportunities (U.S. Department of Education, 2016; Vilorio, 2014).

Given the early emergence and persistence of gaps in mathematical knowledge, it is essential to identify the experiences that relate to children's early mathematical development, and to find ways to provide all children with these positive mathematics-related experiences. To that end, in this chapter, we focus on how parents can effectively support children's early mathematical development, and the factors that can undermine this support, notably parents' math anxiety—the fear and apprehension of doing mathematics (Ashcraft, 2002; Hembree, 1990; Richardson & Suinn, 1972)—and its intergenerational effects on children's mathematical learning and attitudes. We then provide suggestions for how math anxious parents can best support their children's mathematical learning.

THE IMPORTANCE OF EARLY PARENT MATHEMATICS ENGAGEMENT

Because differences in mathematical knowledge emerge before schooling even begins, it stands to reason that the supports parents provide—or do not provide—to their children may play a role in these differences. In fact, the amount and quality of number talk that parents engage in with their children at an early age, controlling for other talk and family socioeconomic background, predicts children's attainment of early foundational mathematical concepts, such as understanding the cardinal principle (e.g., when counting a set of objects, the last number in the counting sequence names the quantity for that set; Levine, Suriyakham, Rowe, Huttenlocher, & Gunderson, 2010). Further, the spatial talk parents engage in with their children—for example, talk about dimensions (e.g., "tall," "short"), shape (e.g., "rectangle," "triangle"), and spatial features (e.g., "straight," "curved")—supports children's own spatial language production and their performance on nonverbal spatial tasks (Pruden, Levine, & Huttenlocher, 2011). In addition to these aspects of math talk, the frequency and variety of mathematical activities in which parents engage their children at home are also related to later mathematical knowledge (e.g., LeFevre et al., 2009; Skwarchuk, Sowinski, & LeFevre, 2014).

Although parents serve as a child's first mathematics teacher, making them undeniably critical to the development of their children's mathematical knowledge prior to entering school, parental involvement remains an essential component of children's educational achievement even once formal schooling begins (e.g., Fan & Chen, 2001; Hill & Taylor, 2004; Jeynes, 2003, 2005). However, parents' engagement in mathematics-related activities with their children can have unintended negative consequences. For example, there is much variability in the quality of mothers' scaffolding of material when helping their children with homework (Hyde, Else-Quest, Alibali, Knuth, & Romberg, 2006), and low quality mathematics interactions might lead children to develop negative attitudes about mathematics, and may even confuse them about the mathematical concepts and procedures they are learning in school (Maloney, Ramirez, Gunderson, Levine, & Beilock, 2015).

Although different factors contribute to the varying quality of parent-child mathematics interactions (e.g., mathematical ability, time, interest, etc.), research most strongly implicates parental attitudes, such as parents' expectations for their children's success in mathematics, and the value (or importance) they place on the material being studied as having the largest effect on children's learning in mathematics (e.g., Grolnick & Slowiaczek, 1994; Hill & Tyson, 2009). Over the past several years, we have explored the impact of another parent attitude, math anxiety, on parent-child mathematics interactions.

WHAT IS MATH ANXIETY?

Math anxiety has implications both in academic settings, such as taking a mathematics test, and in everyday settings, such as calculating a tip at a restaurant (Ashcraft, 2002; Ashcraft, Krause, & Hopko, 2007; Ashcraft & Moore, 2009). People around the world experience math anxiety (Foley et al., 2017), and as much as 20% of the U.S. population, including nearly half of community college students, is estimated to experience high levels of math anxiety (Eden, Heine, & Jacobs, 2013; Sprute & Beilock, 2016). Of note, the occurrence of math anxiety tends to be higher among females than males, with this sex difference emerging by sixth grade (Hembree, 1990). Generally, math anxiety is not thought of as a binary attribute, but rather is measured as a continuous variable, by asking people to rate how anxious various mathematics-related experiences make them feel (ranging from "not at all anxious" to "very much anxious"; see Box 1 for examples of math anxiety scales). Many people may experience some anxiety about mathematics in specific situations but still fall at the lower end overall on a measure of math anxiety (see Box 1).

Math anxiety is evident as early as first grade (e.g., Harari, Vukovic, & Bailey, 2013; Ramirez, Gunderson, Levine, & Beilock, 2013; see Box 1 for example of a math anxiety scale used with children), increases across schooling (Hembree, 1990), and is linked to poor performance in mathematics (Ashcraft, 2002). Although experimental evidence shows that math anxiety is causally linked to lower mathematical performance, this may also be a bidirectional relationship, with lower mathematical performance leading to increased math anxiety (Beilock, Schaeffer, & Rozek, 2017; Gunderson, Park, Maloney, Beilock, & Levine, 2018).

Although math anxiety is associated with poor performance in mathematics, it is not simply a proxy for poor mathematical ability (Faust, Ashcraft, & Fleck, 1996; Jamieson, Peters, Greenwood, & Altose, 2016; Park, Ramirez, & Beilock, 2014). In fact, math anxiety exists across the

Box 1.
How is Math Anxiety Measured?

Math anxiety is measured using a questionnaire where each item represents a situation that may make a respondent feel anxious. Questions include highly academic scenarios such as "How do you feel when getting ready to study for a math test?" or describe everyday situations like, "How do you feel when reading a cash register receipt after your purchase?" Respondents are asked to rate the level of anxiety they associate with each item, from 1 ("not at all") to 5 ("very much").

Selected scales available to measure math anxiety in adults:

- The Mathematics Anxiety Rating Scale (MARS; Suinn, 1972), a 98-item instrument, was among the first instruments developed to assess math anxiety.

- An abbreviated version, the Short-Mathematics Anxiety Rating Scale (sMARS) was developed by Alexander and Martray in 1989. This scale contains 25 items, making it less cumbersome to use than its longer counterpart.

- Most recently, the Single Item Math Anxiety (SIMA) Scale, which is highly correlated with the sMARS, was developed by Núñez-Peña, Guilera, and Suárez-Pellicioni (2014). As indicated by its name, this scale contains only one item: "On a scale of 1 to 10, how math anxious are you?" The anchors for the scale are 1 (not anxious) and 10 (very anxious).

For children, math anxiety questionnaires have been adapted to reflect the mathematics-related situations children encounter in their lives or in school. One such scale, the C-MAQ (Ramirez, Gunderson, Levine, & Beilock, 2013), was designed for use with first and second grade students. Questions include things like: "How do you feel when getting your math book and seeing all the numbers in it?" or "How do you feel when figuring out if you have enough money to buy a candy bar and a soft drink?" Children are then asked to indicate on a smiley-face scale (shown below) how anxious each situation would make them feel.

Very, very
anxious

Not anxious
at all

spectrum of mathematical achievement—even people highly competent in mathematics can be highly anxious about mathematics (e.g., Foley et al., 2017). Further, interventions that ameliorate math anxiety can increase mathematical achievement for math anxious individuals without teaching individuals any additional mathematics (e.g., Park, Ramirez, & Beilock, 2014), indicating that math anxiety is not just about low mathematical ability.

One prominent theory about the relationship between math anxiety and mathematical performance is that the fears and negative emotions that math anxious individuals experience in mathematics-related situations use up cognitive resources, such as working memory, that might otherwise be used on the mathematical task, leading to poor performance (Beilock et al., 2017). Working memory, the ability to keep track of short-term information, may be particularly important when it comes to solving mathematics questions that require holding intermediate steps in mind and computing solutions (Park et al., 2014). Counterintuitively, the negative effects of math anxiety are greatest in individuals with high working memory, and there is evidence that this math anxiety by working memory interaction holds both around the world (Foley et al., 2017) and across ages (Ramirez et al., 2013). We have found that as early as first and second grade, math anxious children who were high in working memory performed more poorly than their high working memory peers who were not math anxious on calculation problems (Ramirez et al., 2013). This was at least partly because they were less likely to use advanced problem-solving strategies—decomposition and retrieval—than children with high working memory who were not math anxious. Instead, these high working memory-high math anxious students frequently deployed the more basic, error-prone strategies (e.g., counting) used by low working memory students (Ramirez, Chang, Maloney, Levine, & Beilock, 2016), likely because their cognitive resources were being taxed by their feelings of anxiety. Taken together, these findings show that math anxiety can compromise the potential of high working memory children to perform at high levels in mathematics. At the same time, when individuals underperform in mathematics, this may increase their anxiety (Foley et al., 2017; Gunderson et al., 2018; Levine, Gunderson, Maloney, Ramirez, & Beilock, 2015). Thus, math anxiety prevents individuals from demonstrating their true ability through a vicious cycle in which math anxiety leads to poor mathematical performance and the poor mathematical performance leads to increased math anxiety.

Math anxiety does not only impact performance on mathematical tasks, it also affects behavior outside of academic situations, leading math anxious individuals to avoid situations where they might encounter mathematics (Ashcraft, 2002; Ashcraft et al., 2007; Hembree, 1990; Maloney & Beilock,

2012). Math anxious individuals tend to take fewer mathematics classes than their non-math anxious counterparts, avoid mathematics-related majors and careers, and may even avoid seemingly mundane activities like calculating a tip at a restaurant (Chipman, Krantz, & Silver, 1992). When math anxious individuals do take mathematics classes, they tend to perform worse in the class than those who are less math anxious (Ashcraft, 2002; Hembree, 1990; Ma, 1999).

Although math anxiety has been shown to negatively affect the mathematical performance of the individuals who suffer from it, we have found that math anxiety also can have intergenerational effects. For example, work in our lab has shown that students of math anxious teachers learn less mathematics over the school year than students of non-math anxious teachers (Beilock, Gunderson, Ramirez, & Levine, 2010). We have also shown that parents' math anxiety matters for students' mathematical learning. Although parents' homework help is generally assumed to be beneficial to students, this is not necessarily the case when parents are high in math anxiety, in part because they are less able to support their children doing mathematics in the home (Herts et al., 2017). In fact, we have found that frequent mathematics homework help to first and second graders by high math anxious parents predicts less mathematical learning over the first or second grade school year both compared to children of high math anxious parents who help less and compared to children of low math anxious parents, regardless of their level of help. Importantly, this relation held controlling for children's mathematical knowledge at the beginning of the school year as well as children's own math anxiety (Maloney et al., 2015). This suggests that the homework help of well-meaning parents can backfire perhaps because their math anxiety makes their homework help less effective even for the relatively basic mathematics homework children are asked to complete in early elementary school. Furthermore, we have found that when parents are math anxious, they provide less number talk to their preschool children, particularly the kinds of number talk that may be most important in driving learning (Berkowitz, Gibson, Monahan, & Levine, 2017; Eason, Nelson, Leonard, Dearing, & Levine, 2017). Together, these findings suggest that math anxiety could lead to differences in both the quantity and quality of teacher-student and parent-child mathematics interactions, and implicate these differences in children's mathematical learning.

Because math anxiety has negative effects both for the math anxious individual and for those in their care, math anxiety can have a broad and reverberating impact. It is important to develop interventions that support both math anxious individuals, as well as the children who interact with these individuals. The next section will delve into recent interventions that hold promise for addressing these issues.

COPING WITH MATH ANXIETY

Researchers have started to develop interventions and supports that can ameliorate the negative impacts of math anxiety. Although interventions that target students directly, including expressive writing tasks, have proven effective in helping math anxious students (Hines, Brown, & Myran, 2016; Jamieson et al., 2016; Park et al., 2014), in this section we focus on interventions that target parents with preschool and school age children. Finding ways to support the home mathematics environment of children with math anxious parents may help ensure that young children have the tools they need to succeed in mathematics. Currently, many parent-targeted interventions are geared toward encouraging parents to increase their engagement in mathematical activities and their math talk with children at home. However, research suggests that this approach may not work if parents feel pushed into doing activities that make them anxious, or feel ill-equipped to guide an interaction with their child, as their involvement is less likely to be sustained, and therefore will have minimal positive effects on children's mathematical learning (Grolnick, 2016; Katz, Kaplan, & Buzukashvily, 2011). Math anxious parents will likely be unhappy during these interactions, creating a negative experience for the child, which could limit the value of the interaction in supporting the child's learning (e.g., Maloney et al., 2015). Creating opportunities for parents to learn or to review the concepts their children are learning in school may boost their feelings of self-efficacy when it comes to engaging their children in mathematics at home. This may especially be true when students are learning to do mathematics in ways that are unfamiliar to parents, a common complaint of parents whose children are learning mathematics with the framework of the Common Core State Standards.

Our research has focused on ways to increase the quality of parent-child mathematics interactions by providing semistructured, age appropriate, and engaging ways for them to engage in mathematical thinking and problem solving together. For example, in one study, we gave parents in the experimental group number books to read with their preschool-aged children and gave parents in the control group similar books that focused on other adjectives (e.g., fuzzy, fluffy). We found that children whose parents were in the number book condition learned the meanings of individual number words, a process that can span months to even years, much faster than expected (i.e., that "two" refers to sets containing two objects), whereas this was not true of the children in the control group (Gibson, Gunderson, & Levine, 2015). Although this study did not focus specifically on parents with math anxiety, this finding suggests that enabling all parents to engage in number talk with their children through the structured environment of picture books can help promote children's understanding of cardinality.

In another randomized controlled study, we looked at whether giving parents a structured, engaging, and low-pressure way to talk to their children about mathematics might help promote children's mathematical learning, especially for children whose parents are math anxious (Berkowitz et al., 2015). In this study, some families were provided with a mathematics app called *Bedtime Math* in the fall of first grade and others were provided with a similar control app focused on reading with their children. Parents in both the experimental and control groups were encouraged to use the app at least four times a week. The app featured daily topical word problems based on holidays and current events, and the passages were developmentally appropriate for young children (see Box 2 for a sample mathematics passage and questions).

At the end of the school year, we found that in the control group, children of highly math anxious parents learned less mathematics than children of lower math anxious parents, consistent with previous findings (e.g., Maloney et al., 2015). However, when families received the mathematics app, children of math anxious parents learned as much as children of low math anxious parents, even though parents' own math anxiety did not change over the course of the year. This finding suggests that math anxious parents might be engaging in mathematics less – or in less effective ways—compared to non-math anxious parents. Further, it shows that with the help of structured mathematical activities—like those provided in the mathematics app or other guided activities that parents and children can do together—this difference can be negated as math-anxious parents engage their children more frequently and effectively in mathematics.

Parents can also help to promote positive motivational attitudes about mathematics by emphasizing and communicating the personal relevance of mathematics to their children (Rozek, Hyde, Svoboda, Hulleman, & Harackiewicz, 2015; Rozek, Svoboda, Harackiewicz, Hulleman, & Hyde, 2017). In a recent study with high school students, one group of parents was given materials and access to a website that explained the relevance of mathematics for their teenagers' everyday lives (e.g., video games, cooking, art, sports, cell phones) and also future careers, while another group of parents was not given any additional materials. Results showed that children of parents with the mathematics-relevance materials took more optional mathematics courses in high school and scored better on the mathematics section of the ACT than children whose parents were in the control group (Rozek et al., 2017). Talking about the relevance of mathematics to young children, such as highlighting how mathematics can be used in everyday activities like setting the table, cooking or recognizing shapes is an approach that holds promise for fostering children's interest and achievement in mathematics from early ages (Harackiewicz, Smith, & Priniski, 2016; Vandermaas-Peeler, Boomgarden, Finn, & Pittard, 2012).

Box 2.

Whipped Cream Gone Wild: Sample Passage and Questions From the *Bedtime Math* App

Whipped cream was invented about 500 years ago, and is credited to a bunch of guys with long unpronounceable Italian and French names. But what made them think to whip up cream in the first place? Did they know what would happen? Never mind that there was no electricity back then—they had to whip it by hand. Luckily, it was worth the effort.

Selected scales available to measure math anxiety in adults:

Whipping air bubbles into cream makes it take up a lot more "volume," or space. In the Bedtime Learning Together test kitchen, 1 cup of heavy cream generated 3 cups of whipped cream. With something as important as dessert, that's a key fact.

Wee ones: If you can whip 2 cups of heavy cream into 6 cups of whipped cream, how many cups of air did you whip into it?

Little kids: If you're making whipped cream for a party, and 1 cup of heavy cream makes 3 cups of whipped cream, how much whipped cream does 6 cups make?

Big kids: If a can of whipped cream holds 6 cups, and when you open it, it kind of explodes and squirts 1 1/2 cups on you, how much is left in the can?

Wee ones: 4 cups of air.

Little kids: 18 cups of whipped cream.

Big kids: 4 1/2 cups.

Thus, with the right materials, parents can help their young children learn basic mathematical concepts at early ages and help their older children stay motivated in mathematics in high school.

IMPLICATIONS AND RECOMMENDATIONS

Research on math anxiety has primarily focused on what it is and how it relates to individuals' performance. However, it is also important to consider the intergenerational effects of math anxiety, and the types of interventions that can be developed to cut the transmission of low mathematical achievement and negative attitudes toward mathematics from adults to the children in their lives. Although parents are encouraged to be more involved in their children's academic work, this can be a daunting (and ineffective) directive for those who suffer from math anxiety. Taking individual attitudes as well as pedagogical and content knowledge into consideration when developing home and school interventions, and constructing professional development for teachers as well as supports for parents are critical components to ensuring increased mathematical achievement and positive attitudes toward mathematics in children.

Given the evidence suggesting an intergenerational link between parents' math anxiety and children's mathematical achievement (Berkowitz et al., 2015; Maloney et al., 2015; Soni & Kumari, 2015), it is critical to create ways to support the mathematics interactions that children have with the adults in their lives. This can be done in a variety of different ways, either through providing models of positive and constructive mathematics interactions or by literally providing a script (as in the case of the mathematics story books and mathematics apps) to guide interactions. Interventions that focus on providing guidance for parents and teachers to praise children in a way that supports the development of growth mindsets through process praise ("Good job on that problem!") rather than person praise ("You're good at math!"), or helping them talk to children about how mathematics is used in everyday life (e.g., cooking, shopping, creating a schedule), may also play an important role in supporting children's mathematical achievement and attitudes toward mathematics (e.g., Gunderson et al., 2017). Teaching parents to avoid saying things like "Math is hard," or otherwise sharing their negative views towards mathematics, and to approach mathematics as an exciting, surmountable challenge, will help children develop positive attitudes towards mathematics as well. Whether this type of support is dispensed through websites (e.g., creating video content to post on YouTube), apps (such as the *Bedtime Math* app discussed here), or even through community mathematics nights, it has the potential for large impacts.

Hopefully, with a little guidance, our opening example of a parent-child mathematics interaction can become more positive and encouraging. Imagine instead …

A mother notices her child struggling with mathematics homework and sits down to help her.

"Let's try to figure this question out together!" she exclaims.

The mother looks at the worksheet and begins to talk through the concepts addressed on the worksheet. She writes out a question, and lets her child attempt to solve it on her own, providing encouragement and guidance when necessary. Once the child understands the main concept, she goes on to solve the questions on the homework sheet. Before they know it, the worksheet is done.

"You did a great job!" says mom. "All your hard work in math is really paying off. I'm excited to see what you learn next!"

REFERENCES

Alexander, L., & Martray, C. (1989). The development of an abbreviated version of the Mathematics Anxiety Rating Scale. *Measurement and Evaluation in Counseling and Development, 22*, 143–150.

Ashcraft, M. H. (2002). Math anxiety: Personal, educational, and cognitive consequences. *Current Directions in Psychological Science, 11*, 181–185. doi:https://doi.org/10.1111/1467-8721.00196

Ashcraft, M. H., Krause, J. A., & Hopko, D. R. (2007). Is math anxiety a mathematical learning disability? In D. B. Berch & M. M. M. Mazzocco (Eds.), *Why is math so hard for some children? The nature and origins of mathematical learning difficulties and disabilities* (pp. 329–348). Baltimore, MD: Brookes.

Ashcraft, M. H., & Moore, M. A. (2009). Mathematics anxiety and the affective drop in performance. *Journal of Psychoeducational Assessment, 27*, 197–205. doi:https://doi.org/10.1177/0734282908330580

Beilock, S. L., Gunderson, E. A., Ramirez, G., & Levine, S. C. (2010). Female teachers' math anxiety affects girls' math achievement. *Proceedings of the National Academy of Sciences, USA, 107*(5), 1060–1063. doi: 10.1073/pnas.0910967107

Beilock, S. L., Schaeffer, M. W., & Rozek, C. S. (2017). Understanding and addressing performance anxiety. In A. J. Elliot, C. S. Dweck, & D. S. Yeager (Eds.), *Handbook of competence and motivation: Theory and application* (2nd ed.). New York, NY: Guilford Press.

Berkowitz, T., Gibson, D., Monahan, J., & Levine, S. C. (2017, April). *Math anxiety and parents' use of number words with their children.* Paper presented at the biennial meeting of the Society for Research on Child Development, Austin, TX.

Berkowitz, T., Schaeffer, M. W., Maloney, E. A., Peterson, L., Gregor, C., Levine, S. C., & Beilock, S. L. (2015). Math at home adds up to achievement in school. *Science, 350*(6257), 196–198. doi:10.1126/science.aac7427

Chipman, S., Krantz, D. H., & Silver, R. (1992). Mathematics anxiety and science careers among able college women. *Psychological Science, 3*(5), 292–295. doi:https://doi.org/10.1111/j.1467-9280.1992.tb00675.x

Clements, D. H., & Sarama, J. (2007). Effects of a preschool mathematics curriculum: Summative research on the Building Blocks Project. *Journal for Research in Mathematics Education, 38*(2), 136–163. doi:10.2307/30034954

Duncan, G. J., Dowsett, C. J., Claessens, A., Magnuson, K., Huston, A. C., … Japel, C. (2007). School readiness and later achievement. *Developmental Psychology, 43*(6), 1428–1446. doi:10.1037/0012-1649.43.6.1428

Eden, C., Heine, A., & Jacobs, A. (2013). Mathematics anxiety and its development in the course of formal schooling: A review. *Psychology, 4*, 27-35. doi:10.4236/psych.2013.46A2005

Entwisle, D. R., & Alexander, K. L. (1990). Beginning school math competence: Minority and majority comparisons. *Child Development, 61*(2), 454–471. doi:10.2307/1131107

Eason, S. H., Nelson, A., Leonard, S., Dearing, E., & Levine, S. C. (2017, April). *Parents' math anxiety and talk about numbers during pretend play with preschoolers.* Paper presented at the biennial meeting of the Society for Research on Child Development, Austin, TX.

Fan, X., & Chen, M. (2001). Parental involvement and students' academic achievement: A meta-analysis. *Educational Psychology Review, 13*(1), 1–22. doi:https://doi.org/10.1023/A:100904881

Faust, M.W., Ashcraft, M. H., & Fleck, D. E. (1996). Mathematics anxiety effects in simple and complex addition. *Mathematical Cognition, 2,* 25–62. doi:http://dx.doi.org/10.1080/135467996387534

Foley, A. E., Herts, J. B., Borgonovi, F., Guerriero, S., Levine, S. C. & Beilock, S. L. (2017). The math anxiety-performance link: A global phenomenon. *Current Directions in Psychological Science, 26*(1), 52–58. doi:10.1177/0963721416672463

Gibson, D. J., Gunderson, E. A., & Levine, S. C. (2015, March). *Number word learning: A parent-driven training study.* Talk presented at the biennial meeting of the Society for Research in Child Development, Philadelphia, PA.

Griffin, S. A., Case, R., & Siegler, R. S. (1994). Rightstart: Providing the central conceptual prerequisites for first formal learning of arithmetic to students at risk for school failure. In K. McGilly (Ed.), *Classroom lessons: Integrating cognitive theory and classroom practice* (pp. 24–49). Cambridge, MA: MIT Press.

Grolnick, W. S. (2016). Parental involvement and children's academic motivation and achievement. In W. C. Liu, J. C. K. Wang, & R. M. Ryan (Eds.), *Building autonomous learners: Perspectives from research and practice using self-determination theory* (pp. 169–183). Singapore: Springer.

Grolnick, W. S., & Slowiaczek, M. L. (1994). Parents' involvement in children's schooling: A multidimensional conceptualization and motivational model. *Child Development, 65*(1), 237–252. doi:10.2307/1131378

Gunderson, E. A., Sorhagen, N. S., Gripshover, S. J., Dweck, C. S., Goldin-Meadow, S., & Levine, S. C. (2017). Parent praise to toddlers predicts fourth grade academic achievement via children's incremental mindsets. *Developmental Psychology, 54*(3), 397–409. doi:10.1037/dev0000444

Gunderson, E. A., Park, C., Maloney, E. A., Beilock, S. L., & Levine, S. C. (2018). Reciprocal relations among motivational frameworks, math anxiety, and math achievement in early elementary school. *Journal of Cognition and Development, 19*(1). doi:https://doi.org 10.1080/15248372.2017.1421538

Gunderson, E. A., Park, D., Maloney, E. A., Beilock, S. L. & Levine, S. C. (in press). Reciprocal relations among motivation frameworks, math anxiety, and math achievement in early elementary school.

Harackiewicz, J. M., Smith, J. L., & Priniski, S. J. (2016). Interest matters: The importance of promoting interest in education. *Policy Insights from the Behavioral and Brain Sciences, 3,* 220–227. doi:https://doi.org/10.1177/2372732216655542

Harari, R. R., Vukovic, R. K., & Bailey, S. P. (2013). Mathematics anxiety in young children: An exploratory study. *Learning, Instruction, and Cognition, 81*(4). 538–555. doi:http://dx.doi.org/10.1080/00220973.2012.727888

Hembree, R. (1990). The nature, effects and relief of mathematics anxiety. *Journal for Research in Mathematics Education, 21*(1), 33–46. doi:10.2307/749455

Herts, J. B., Rozek, C. S., Schaeffer, M. W., Berkowitz, T., Stallings, W., Beilock, S. L., & Levine, S. C. (2017, May). *Math anxious parents provide lower quality math instruction.* Poster presented at the Association for Psychological Science annual conference, Boston, MA.

Hill, N. E., & Taylor, L. C. (2004). Parental school involvement and children's academic achievement: Pragmatics and issues. *Current Directions in Psychological Science, 13*, 161–164. doi:https://doi.org/10.1111/j.0963-7214.2004.00298.x

Hill, N. E., & Tyson, D. F. (2009). Parental involvement in middle school: A meta-analytic assessment of the strategies that promote achievement. *Developmental Psychology, 45*(3), 740–763. doi:10.1037/a0015362

Hines, C. L., Brown, N. W., & Myran, S. (2016). The effects of expressive writing on general and mathematics anxiety for a sample of high school students. *Education, 137*(1), 39–45.

Hyde, J. S., Else-Quest, N. M., Alibali, M. W., Knuth, E., & Romberg, T. (2006). Mathematics in the home: Homework practices and mother-child interactions doing mathematics. *Journal of Mathematical Behavior, 25*, 136–152. doi:10.1016/j.jmathb.2006.02.003

Jamieson, J. P., Peters, B. J., Greenwood, E. J., & Altose, A. J. (2016). Reappraising stress arousal improves performance and reduces evaluations anxiety in classroom exam situations. *Social Psychological and Personality Science, 7*(6), 579–587. doi:https://doi.org/10.1177/1948550616644656

Jeynes, W. H. (2003). A meta-analysis: The effects of parental involvement on minority children's academic achievement. *Education and Urban Society, 35*, 202–218. doi:https://doi.org/10.1177/0013124502239392

Jeynes, W. H. (2005). A meta-analysis of the relation of parental involvement to urban elementary school student academic achievement. *Urban Education, 40*(3), 237–269. doi:https://doi.org/10.1177/0042085905274540

Jordan, N. C., & Levine, S. C. (2009). Socio-economic variation, number competence, and mathematical learning difficulties in young children. *Developmental Disabilities Research Reviews, 15*, 60–68. doi:10.1002/ddrr.46

Katz, I., Kaplan, A., & Buzukashvily, T. (2011). The role of parents' motivation in students' autonomous motivation for doing homework. *Learning and Individual Differences, 21*, 376–386. doi:https://doi.org/10.1016/j.lindif.2011.04.001

Klibanoff, R. S., Levine, S. C., Huttenlocher, J., Vasilyeva, M., & Hedges, L. V. (2006). Preschool children's mathematical knowledge: The effect of teacher "math talk". *Developmental Psychology, 42*(1), 59–69. doi:10.1037/0012-1649.42.1.59

LeFevre, J.-A., Skwarchuk, S.-L., Smith-Chant, B. L., Fast, L., Kamawar, D., & Bisanz, J. (2009). Home numeracy experiences and children's math performance in the early school years. *Canadian Journal of Behavioural Science, 41*(2), 55–66. doi:http://dx.doi.org/10.1037/a0014532

Levine, S. C., Gunderson, E. A., & Huttenlocher, J. (2011). Number development in context: Variations in home and school input during the preschool years. In N. Stein & S. Raudenbush (Eds.), *Developmental cognitive science goes to school* (pp. 189–202). New York, NY: Taylor and Francis.

Levine, S. C., Gunderson, E. A., Maloney, E., Ramirez, G., & Beilock, S. (2015, March). *The role of parents in young children's math learning: Cognitive and emotional factors.* Paper presented at the biennial meeting of the Society for Research on Child Development, Philadelphia, PA.

Levine, S. C., Suriyakham, L., Rowe, M., Huttenlocher, J., & Gunderson, E. (2010). What counts in the development of children's number knowledge? *Developmental Psychology, 46*(5), 1309–1319. doi:10.1037/a0019671

Ma, X. (1999). A meta-analysis of the relationship between anxiety toward mathematics and achievement in mathematics. *Journal for Research in Mathematics Education*, *30*(5), 520–540. doi:10.2307/749772

Maloney, E. A., & Beilock, S. L. (2012). Math anxiety: Who has it, why it develops, and how to guard against it. *Trends in Cognitive Sciences*, *16*, 404–406. doi:10.1016/j.tics.2012.06.008

Maloney, E. A., Ramirez, G., Gunderson, E. A., Levine, S. C., & Beilock, S. L. (2015). Intergenerational effects of low math achievement and high math anxiety. *Psychological Science*, *26*(9), 1480–1488. doi:10.1177/0956797615592630

National Assessment of Educational Progress. (2015). *The nation's report card-2015; 4th and 8th grade mathematics assessments*. Retrieved from https://www.nationsreportcard.gov/reading_math_2015/#mathematics?grade=4

Núñez-Peña, M. I., Guilera, G., & Suárez-Pellicioni, M. (2014). The single-item math anxiety scale: An alternative way of measuring mathematical anxiety. *Journal of Psychoeducational Assessment*, *32*(4), 306–317. doi:https://doi.org/10.1177/0734282913508528

Organisation for Economic Co-operation and Development (OECD). (2016). *Country note: Key findings from PISA 2015 for the United States*. Retrieved from https://www.oecd.org/pisa/pisa-2015-United-States.pdf

Park, D., Ramirez, G., & Beilock, S. L. (2014). The role of expressive writing in math anxiety. *Journal of Experimental Psychology: Applied*, *20*(2), 103–111. doi:10.1037/xap0000013

Pruden, S. M., Levine, S. C., & Huttenlocher, J. (2011). Children's spatial thinking: Does talk about the spatial world matter? *Developmental Science*, *14*(6), 1417–1430. doi:10.1111/j.1467-7687.2011.01088.x

Ramirez, G., Chang, H., Maloney, E. A., Levine, S. C., & Beilock. S. L. (2016). On the relationship between math anxiety and math achievement in early elementary school: The role of problem solving strategies. *Journal of Experimental Child Psychology*, *141*, 83–100. doi: https://doi.org/10.1016/j.jecp.2015.07.014

Ramirez, G., Gunderson, E. A., Levine, S. C., & Beilock, S. L. (2013). Math anxiety, working memory and math achievement in early elementary school. *Journal of Cognition and Development*, *14*(2), 187–202. doi:10.3389/fpsyg.2016.00042

Reardon, S. F. (2011). The widening academic achievement gap between the rich and the poor: New evidence and possible explanations. In R. Murnane & G. Duncan (Eds.) *Whither opportunity? Rising inequality and the uncertain life chances of low-income children* (pp. 91–116). New York, NY: Russell Sage Foundation Press.

Richardson, F. C., & Suinn, R. M. (1972). The mathematics anxiety rating scale: Psychometric data. *Journal of Counseling Psychology*, *19*(6), 551–554. doi:http://dx.doi.org/10.1037/h0033456

Rozek, C. S., Hyde, J. S., Svoboda, R. C., Hulleman, C. S., & Harackiewicz, J. M. (2015). Gender differences in the effects of a utility-value intervention to help parents motivate adolescents in mathematics and science. *Journal of Educational Psychology*, *107*(1), 195–206. doi:http://dx.doi.org/10.1037/a0036981

Rozek, C. S., Svoboda, R. C., Harackiewicz, J. M., Hulleman, C. S., & Hyde, J. S. (2017). Utility-value intervention with parents increases students' STEM preparation and career pursuit. *Proceedings of the National Academy of Sciences, USA, 114*(5), 909–914. doi:10.1073/pnas.1607386114

Skwarchuk, S. L., Sowinski, C., & LeFevre, J. A. (2014). Formal and informal home learning activities in relation to children's early numeracy and literacy skills: The development of a home numeracy model. *Journal of Experimental Child Psychology, 121*, 63–84. doi:https://doi.org/10.1016/j.jecp.2013.11.006

Soni, A., & Kumari, S. (2015). The role of parental math attitude in their children math achievement. *International Journal of Applied Sociology, 5*(4), 159–163. doi:10.5923/j.ijas.20150504.01

Sprute, L., & Beilock, S. L. (2016). Math anxiety in community college students. *MathAMATYC Educator, 7*, 39–45.

Starkey, P., Klein, A., & Wakeley, A. (2004). Enhancing young children's mathematical knowledge through a pre-kindergarten mathematics intervention. *Early Childhood Research Quarterly, 19*(1), 99–120. doi:https://doi.org/10.1016/j.ecresq.2004.01.002

Suinn, R. M. (1972). *Mathematics Anxiety Rating Scale (MARS)*. Fort Collins, CO: Rocky Mountain Behavioral Sciences Institute.

U.S. Department of Education, Office of Innovation and Improvement. (2016). *STEM 2026: A vision for innovation in STEM Education*. Washington, DC. Retrieved from https://innovation.ed.gov/files/2016/09/AIR-STEM2026_Report_2016.pdf

Vandermaas-Peeler, M., Boomgarden, E., Finn, L., & Pittard, C. (2012). Parental support of numeracy during a cooking activity with four-year-olds. *International Journal of Early Years Education, 20*(1), 78–93. doi:http://dx.doi.org/10.1080/09669760.2012.663237

Vilorio, D. (2014, March). STEM 101: Intro to tomorrow's jobs. *Occupational Outlook Quarterly, Bureau of Labor Statistics*. Retrieved from https://www.bls.gov/career-outlook/2014/spring/art01.pdf

CHAPTER 3

LISTENING FOR STRENGTHS IN DIVERSE FAMILIES' CONVERSATIONS ABOUT SCIENCE

Graciela Solis and Maureen Callanan

Educators and education researchers have long argued for the importance of considering students' diverse cultural experiences when designing classroom practices and curricula (González, Andrade, Civil, & Moll, 2001; Gutiérrez, Baquedano-López, & Tejada, 1999; Heath, 1983; Lee, 2006). Science, technology, engineering, and mathematics (STEM) education is an important case in point. The Next Generation Science Standards (NGSS) emphasize that educators should connect school science to students' out-of-school experiences in the home and community contexts to support their engagement in scientific and engineering practices (National Research Council, 2012). Studies have shown that informal parent-child science interactions are opportunities for developing everyday critical thinking practices, even in very young children (Callanan & Jipson, 2001; Haden et al., 2014), and yet we know relatively little about these conversations in diverse families, particularly in the growing population of Latino families in the United States.

Promising Practices for Engaging Families in STEM Learning, pp. 35–48
Copyright © 2018 by Information Age Publishing
All rights of reproduction in any form reserved.

At the same time, focusing on cultural differences also has the potential to trigger unspoken and mistaken beliefs. However well-meaning, efforts to identify how families differ in their everyday cultural practices can often activate deficit assumptions. In this chapter, we provide some background on the problem of deficit assumptions and discuss potential implications for Latino children in science classrooms. We then discuss findings from two studies including Mexican-heritage children and families, where we have shown that common deficit assumptions are incorrect. Counterexamples such as these may help to uncover the problem of deficit thinking and provide evidence to support an alternative strength-based view of diversity.

DEFICIT ASSUMPTIONS ABOUT CULTURAL DIFFERENCES

When cultural variation is studied, there is always a danger that deficit assumptions may emerge. Researchers and educators, like other people, often inadvertently consider their own experience as normative (or "normal"), which can lead to an assumption that any differences in other groups are a sign of something lacking (Medin, Bennis, & Chandler, 2010). In other words, we are naturally biased in how we see the experience of people in cultural groups other than our own. Consider, for example, the widespread assumption that assessments that were developed by and for members of White, middle class, majority Western cultural groups can be accurately used to assess members of different groups, and that these assessments will have the same meaning for different participants. There are many documented cases showing that this approach can lead to incorrect inferences (Cole, 1996; Rogoff, 2003). Just as it would be unfair to test middle-class United States children's number knowledge by asking them to use an abacus that they had never seen, so too is testing children from diverse communities with tools and measures developed only in mainstream U.S. communities.

It is also often much easier for us to see variability within our own cultural group, another attitude that can lead to deficit assumptions (Medin et al., 2010). We know that individuals within our own community have a variety of different values, preferences, and abilities, and yet it is easy for us to see other cultural groups as homogeneous along these same dimensions. Culture should not be viewed as a "trait" or entity within all members of a given group; instead, culture is more accurately seen as a dynamic set of "repertoires of practices" (Gutiérrez & Rogoff, 2003). For example, children's experience of particular everyday family activities is more important for their learning than a group label applied to their community. For this reason, educators should consider particular children's school performance within the context of the cultural practices that they actually engage in with their families.

Researchers and educators who wish to avoid unintended deficit assumptions can use several strategies proposed by Callanan and Waxman (2013), including:

1. **Designing assessments within children's cultural community rather than transplanting assessments from other cultural groups.** For example, asking parents about how their family engages with story-telling is likely to uncover more accurate understanding than giving parents a book and asking them to read it to their child (Solis & Callanan, in press).

2. **Thinking of culture as a multifaceted and dynamic contributor to children's learning.** We know that there are likely to be clusters of many causal factors involved in anything as complex as children's academic performance or cognitive development. And yet, there seems to be a strong tendency, in both research and everyday language, to use causal words such as "influence" when discussing correlational findings. One example is the extensive attention given to the "30 million word gap," where the amount of talk by parents is discussed as a causal factor in children's differential development—even though there is no direct evidence that the number of words parents speak *causes* children's language skills or academic performance to differ (see Miller & Sperry, 2012). Instead, although some studies have found that income level was correlated with the number of words parents spoke, and with children's school performance (Hart & Risley, 1995), income level is also correlated with many other factors, including school resources, children's nutrition, and discrimination, that can negatively impact children's development. Also, a recent study found that parents' speech across several communities did not correlate well with family income (Sperry, Sperry, & Miller, 2015).

3. **Considering the potential harmful impact of deficit assumptions on populations of students and their families.** For example, consider the possible harm that can result from giving parents the message that their cultural practices regarding parenting are wrong or unhealthy.

Some examples in the literature show how deficit models often lead us astray. For example, Rowley and Camacho (2015) point out that standardized test score gaps between Asian students and White students are often as wide as those between White students and Black or Latino students, and yet we seldom hear about the "Asian-White testing gap" as a problem.

When we do hear about the difference between Asian students' test scores and those of White students, it is often focused on questions about whether Asian students' high scores are a sign of unhealthy social development, and not whether White students are academically deficient (Rowley & Camacho, 2015).

A STRENGTHS-BASED PERSPECTIVE ON DIVERSITY

We advocate for strengths-based approaches for interpreting differences. For example, work by Rogoff and her colleagues (Rogoff, 2014) found that children from indigenous Mexican and Guatemalan families showed considerable strengths in learning through keen observation, rather than the direct parent-child verbal teaching experiences favored by European-American families. In a different example, work by Miller, Cho, and Bracey (2005) showed that children from working-class families masterfully justified their views in the context of telling stories of personal events. In contrast to children from middle-income homes who assume that they have the right to state their opinion outright, children from families in working-class households are often guided to defend their points of view through telling stories using artful performance and dramatic language. Although these strengths are recognized in research, Miller et al. (2005) pointed out that children's "fluent participation in personal storytelling will not necessarily be recognized for the strength that it has as they venture beyond home and community" (p. 133). Educators, for instance, might fail to interpret working class children's story-telling as a strength, if they are looking for a style more familiar to them from middle class families (Michaels, 2005).

Commenting on working class children's story-telling, Michaels (2005) provides examples where children from working-class homes did more puzzling about how abstract notions like tilt of the earth related to their own personal experiences, whereas children from middle-class homes tended to just accept these discrepancies without pondering them further. Michaels asked if accepting contradictions without discussion is necessarily better—thus questioning the biased notion apparent in much of the previous research, that White middle-class children's explanations are necessarily normative. Similarly, a number of researchers have called for the need to reframe science in the classroom in order to counteract the power dynamics that lead some children's ideas to be ignored or corrected (Bang, Warren, Rosebery, & Medin, 2012; Calabrese, Barton & Tan, 2010). Bang et al. (2012) argue that science classrooms often implement static ideas about science facts that are different from actual scientists' dynamic and complex ways of thinking, and that "desettling" these ideas can open up new opportunities for learning, especially for students from nondominant backgrounds.

SCIENCE LEARNING IN LATINO FAMILIES

Research that has focused specifically on the academic achievement of Latino children living in the United States, and on science achievement in particular, often reflects a deficit interpretation, even though there are also many studies of the rich and diverse cultural practices that these children bring to the school environment (Bedolla, 2012; Fuller & Garcia Coll, 2010; González et al., 2001). By 2050, Latino children could outnumber non-Latino White children in U.S. public schools (Bedolla, 2012), thus, it is critical to examine not only the school achievement of Latino children, but also how they engage in science-related practices at home, and how those practices can be built upon in the classroom. It is important to first point out that terms like "Latino" and "Hispanic" are often used to describe very diverse and heterogeneous communities. This grouping together of many Latin American groups with distinct practices and belief systems is problematic for many reasons. Though we advocate for focusing on particular communities in research (e.g., Mexican heritage immigrant families), it can also be helpful to (cautiously) consider previous research where Latino communities have been combined in order to identify patterns that hold across different Latino groups.

It has been argued that Latino students' low school achievement is related to educators' preexisting deficit orientations, and this is particularly noticeable within science education (Losey, 1995; Portales & Portales, 2005). For example, teachers often blame Latino parents for their children's lack of success in the classroom, perhaps because educators focus on parents' years of schooling as a sign of their intellectual engagement and parenting involvement (Valencia & Solorzano, 1997). Further, Spanish-speaking Latino students are often taken out of science education courses to learn English, often causing students to fall behind their peers. Lee and Buxton (2013) argue that rather than removing English language learners from science classrooms and treating science and literacy as independent domains, it is more effective for both science learning and English proficiency if learning of content and language are integrated.

Extensive research has demonstrated the effectiveness of building upon students' experiences at home to contextualize classroom curriculum and improve learning (Flores & Manzo, 2012; Gonzalez et al., 2001; Losey, 1995). When we consider very early experiences with science thinking, research on families' conversations about science-related topics have demonstrated variation in opportunities for preschool-aged children to engage in science practices such as carefully observing, using evidence, and seeking explanations (Callanan, Castañeda, Luce, & Martin, 2017; Luce, Callanan, & Smilovic, 2013). These variations could be important for children's later interest in, and engagement with, science.

In order to explore how Latino families engage with these everyday science practices, we need to understand more about their science-related conversations at home. Thus, we next consider two examples of research findings from our lab that counter deficit assumptions regarding science-related talk in Mexican heritage families. Our first case study comes from a diary study of children's "why" questions. Our second case study comes from observational research of family conversations about sinking and floating in a science-related task.

Science Conversations Elicited by Children's "Why" Questions

Children's spontaneous "why" questions give us a window into the ways that children reason causally about a variety of domains, including those that they later learn about in science classrooms (Callanan & Jipson, 2001). For instance, Callanan and Oakes (1992) found that a group of largely European-American children asked many "why" questions at home with parents. However, some research has suggested that children from lower income or non-Western communities may ask fewer "why" questions at home than do middle class children (Gauvain, Munroe, & Beebe, 2013; Tizard & Hughes, 1984). Other work has suggested that Mexican heritage children may ask fewer questions than European American children due to the cultural value of *respeto* [respect] (Delgado-Gaitan, 1994).

In order to explore whether there were differences in question asking across different Mexican heritage communities, we recruited 48 families, each with a 3- to 5-year-old child, from two Mexican descent communities, using a variety of sources including schools, community centers, and apartment complexes. We used parents' years of schooling as a marker of socioeconomic level that correlates with income as well as with a variety of other family practices (Rogoff, 2014). One group of 24 Mexican descent parents had "higher schooling"—these parents had completed at least 12 years of schooling, mostly in the United States, with an average of 14 years. The majority of the parents with higher schooling had immigrated to the U.S. as children, and were fluent in English and Spanish. The second group of 24 Mexican descent parents had completed "basic schooling"— these parents had completed between 2 and 11 years of schooling, mostly in Mexico, with an average of 7 years. The majority of these parents had immigrated to the United States. and spoke Spanish at home. Note that we deliberately use the word "schooling" as a description of parents' experience with the cultural practices of formal schooling, and we draw attention to the fact that parents' "education" and learning take many forms beyond the classroom. In the spirit of avoiding deficit interpretations, we mean no disrespect with the term "basic schooling" and use it only to reflect the difference between cultural practices of formal school and the cultural practices of learning in informal environments (Rogoff, 2014).

Bilingual researchers explained that we were interested in any questions their child asked about "why" or "how" something happened; we asked parents to keep track of their preschool-aged children's "why" questions during everyday activities for two weeks (Callanan, Solis, Perez-Granados, Barajas, & Goldberg, 2017). We then called parents every 2 to 3 days to ask about children's questions and take notes on the conversations. For each episode, parents reported to us the question that initiated the conversation, the context, and their own response, and they gave a summary of the rest of the conversation, all in their preferred language.

We coded the questions as either focused on science topics (e.g., the sun, weather, animal behaviors) or social topics (e.g., reasons for people's actions). We did not find differences in the frequency of children's "why" questions between the two education levels. Further, in both groups of Mexican heritage children, about half of the questions were focused on science-related topics, and both groups asked similar numbers of science-based "why" questions. In addition, we found that parents' responses to the questions were most often causal explanations, and again this pattern held for both groups of parents.

We informally compared the conversations in these two groups of Mexican heritage families to those of 30 mostly middle-income European-American families from an earlier study, who were recruited from a university database (Callanan & Oakes, 1992). Again, the types of conversations did not differ across the two studies. In the diary study with Mexican heritage families, 57% of the questions were followed with causal explanations (Callanan et al., 2017), whereas in the study with mostly European heritage families, parents responded with causal explanations 49% of the time (Callanan & Oakes, 1992).

In other words, despite common deficit assumptions about children whose parents have low income or basic schooling, this study provided strong evidence that the casual conversations children engaged in at home were very similar across these three communities. These findings show that children's question asking did not vary across these groups, nor did parents' answers. In particular, Mexican-heritage children were asking science-related questions at home.

Examples from the diary study illustrate how children from Mexican descent families engaged their parents with both basic and higher schooling in conversations about a variety of science topics in everyday interactions.

Example 1   (parent with more than 12 years of schooling, 5-year-old boy)

Child: Why do fish die outside the water? *(after having gone fishing with his dad)*

Mother: Because water is like oxygen to the fish, and if you take them out they die.

Example 2   (parent with less than 12 years of schooling, 4 year old girl)

Child: Why isn't the white ball up in the sky? (on a night where the moon wasn't visible)

Dad: Because the moon doesn't come out everyday.

Child: Why does it only come out at night?

Dad: The moon only comes out at night so that we can see better.

Example 3   (parent with more than 12 years of schooling, 3-year-old girl)

Child: Why do babies grow? (after visit from baby)

Mother: Because everybody grows up like that, you grew up.

Child: But why?

Mother: Because people, everybody has to grow.

Child: Am I going to grow up like you?

Mother: Yes.

Child: I don't want to grow up!

Example 4   (parent with less than 12 years of schooling, 4-year-old boy)

Child: Why don't fish fly?

Mother: Because fish do not have wings and they only know how to swim in the water.

Example 5   (parent with more than 12 years of schooling, 4-year-old girl)

Child: Why did the dinosaurs die? (Reading a book on dinosaurs)

Mother: For many reasons, there wasn't enough food for them.

Child: No, it's because the planet got cold.

Example 6   (parent with less than 12 years of schooling, 5-year-old girl)

Child: How is it that fish are in the water and they won't drown?

Mother: You were born to be on earth, God made those animals only for water.

Overall, these results demonstrate the presence of complex causal questions in the conversations of children from diverse backgrounds. They show that children from diverse backgrounds express curiosity about science domains, and that parents with varying schooling experience respond with causal explanations. These findings highlight the importance of examining and understanding the home practices of a variety of cultural groups before assuming deficits.

Parent-Child Conversations in a Science-Related Task

Our second example comes from a study focused on exploring conversations during a science-related activity among 40 Mexican-heritage families living in the United States (Siegel, Esterly, Callanan, Wright, & Navarro, 2007; Solis & Callanan, 2016, in press; Tenenbaum & Callanan, 2008). Families were recruited using similar methods described above (i.e., from community centers, apartment complexes) and participated in their language of choice. We videotaped families at home while they engaged in a hybrid science-related game that we designed to bridge between home and school practices. Again, we included two groups of 20 Mexican-heritage families: parents with "higher schooling" had completed an average of 13 years of schooling; most of these parents were born in the U.S. and were bilingual. Those parents with "basic schooling" had completed an average of seven years of formal schooling; most were born in Mexico and immigrated to the United States and spoke Spanish at home.

Families were given a basin of water and a variety of objects, including an empty bottle, a wooden block, a plastic sea animal, and a plastic bracelet. Parent and child were asked to predict together which objects would sink and which would float—two baskets were provided to help them keep track of their predictions. Then they were asked to test their predictions.

Our goal was to identify signs of science practices, like those identified by the NGSS standards, as being crucial to scientific thought in young children. Specifically, we were interested in the ways that parents and children talked about their predictions and their observations. We explored the types of questions asked by both parents and children, and the ways that evidence was considered in testing out their predictions. Although deficit assumptions would lead to expectations that the basic schooling families might be limited in their use of scientific practices, our findings contradicted such assumptions. We found that basic schooling parents collaborated more with their children in testing out their predictions together, and focused more on observing what happened, even when it violated their own predictions. The following example with a 4-year-old boy and his mother illustrates this type of interaction:

Mother:	(observing objects in the water) Fíjate como este no se fue para abajo. (pushes die) Y pensábamos que se iba a ir para abajo. Y la rana. [*(observing objects in the water) Notice how this one did not go to the bottom (pushes die). And we thought it would go to the bottom! And the frog.*]
Child:	Y, todos. [*And all of them.*]
Mother:	Y el d'este, mira. El rabbit también se quedó arriba. [*And this one, look. The rabbit also stayed on top.*]
Child:	Uh-huh.
Mother:	Es que es de madera. Fíjate como esta que está más pesada quedó poquito arriba también (large water-filled bottle). [*That's because it's wood. Notice how this one that's heavier (large water-filled bottle) stayed a little on top, too.*]

This mother points out that an object she had not expected to float had indeed floated. Basic schooling parents often focused on understanding what was happening with the specific objects.

In contrast, the higher schooling parents were more likely to take on the role of teacher, organizing the task, stating general rules, and evaluating their children's performance, but not as likely to comment on their own mistaken predictions. They asked more questions of their children, including open-ended questions, which is one way to encourage children's active participation. The higher schooling mothers also focused on general rules, even though sometimes the rule did not match the evidence that was apparent at the time. For example, while testing out their predictions, this four-year-old seemed confused by an unexpected outcome.

Child:	Mami.... y ... y ... est- ... (takes out frog). [*Mami ... and ... and ... this ... (takes out frog).*]
Mother	No, pero los de plástico se fueron para abajo. [*No, but the plastic ones went down.*]

The mom focused on general rules like "wood floats" and "plastic sinks," but did not acknowledge that the rule was contradicted by the evidence her child was pointing out, in other words, that the plastic frog was floating and thus did not follow her general rule.

Intriguingly, these differences in parents' science talk were accompanied by differences in children's questions. Children in the basic schooling group were more likely to ask conceptual questions, for example about why things sink or float, while children in the higher schooling group were more likely to ask procedural questions, for example about how to play the game (Solis & Callanan, 2016, in press).

In some ways, the higher schooling families match the expectations of what school science eventually looks like. For example, educational practices of assessment through testing seemed to be recognizable in the ways that these parents organized the task. However, it is very intriguing that the basic schooling parents seemed to provide several different types of opportunities for the type of open-ended science inquiry that is encouraged by the NGSS (National Research Council, 2012). Specifically, we found that Mexican-heritage parents in the basic schooling group engaged in evidence-based collaborative inquiry. Using a different approach, the higher schooling parents positioned themselves as teachers, sometimes guiding children toward correct answers. The higher schooling parents also emphasized questions to children, which is one important aspect of scientific inquiry.

CONCLUSIONS

In two case studies, we have shown that deficit assumptions can be misleading. Mexican immigrant parents with basic schooling experience displayed productive engagement in science-related conversations with their young children. In the case of conversations instigated by children's "why" questions, these families engaged in science-related talk in ways that were not different from other families from other backgrounds. In the case of a science-based game, the basic schooling families arguably showed deeper engagement with evidence as defined by the NGSS, while higher schooling families engaged in more questions. In both studies, the young children in basic schooling families defied deficit expectations and demonstrated deep thinking about scientific concepts. As Michaels (2005) and Miller et al. (2005) argued, the next step will be in trying to make these skills and ideas visible to educators and researchers who may see these children through the lens of deficit models. Some very promising preliminary ideas for changing classroom science to better support diverse learners have been documented by Bang et al. (2012) and Calabrese Barton and Tan (2010), as well as McIntyre, Rosebery, and Gonzalez (2001). These ideas fit with broader ideas about science education reform (Hammer & van Zee, 2006), privileging opportunities for students to actively engage with meaningful material and make sense of their observations.

RECOMMENDATIONS FOR
EDUCATORS AND POLICYMAKERS

- Consider your unexamined biases and resist deficit thinking about children from backgrounds different from your own, and consider the power dynamics at play when engaging with families from non-dominant communities.

- Try to keep English language learners in science classrooms and recognize that students learn both language and ways of thinking scientifically in open-ended exploratory science activities—at the same time.
- Create ways for parents and children to engage meaningfully in conversations about nature and science, perhaps in-home discussions about projects in school. For example, if studying astronomy, have children ask their parents about their memories of looking at the stars when they were children.
- Recognize that parents' educational background is not a predictor of their skill in engaging their child in inquiry.

REFERENCES

Bang, M., Warren, B., Rosebery, A., & Medin, D. (2012). Desettling expectations in science education. *Human Development, 55,* 302–318. doi:10.1159/000345322

Bedolla, L. G. (2012). Latino education, civic engagement, and the public good. *Review of Research and Education, 36,* 23–42. doi:10.3102/0091732X11422666

Calabrese Barton, A., & Tan, E. (2010). We be burnin'! Agency, identity, and science learning. *Journal of the Learning Sciences, 19,* 187–229. doi:10.1080/10508400903530044

Callanan, M., Castañeda, C., Luce, M., & Martin, J. (2017). Family science talk in museums: Predicting children's engagement from variations in talk and activity. *Child Development, 88,* 1492–1504. doi:10.1111/cdev.12886

Callanan, M., & Jipson, J. (2001). Explanatory conversations and young children's developing scientific literacy. In K. Crowley, C. Schunn, & T. Okada (Eds.), *Designing for science: Implications from everyday, classroom, and professional settings* (pp. 21–49). Mahwah, NJ: Erlbaum.

Callanan, M., & Oakes, L. (1992). Preschoolers' questions and parents' explanations: Causal thinking in everyday activity. *Cognitive Development, 7,* 213–233. doi:https://doi.org/10.1016/0885-2014(92)90012-G

Callanan, M., Solis, G., Perez-Granados, D., Barajas, N., & Goldberg, J. (2017). Why questions in Mexican-descent children's conversations with parents. Manuscript submitted for publication.

Callanan, M., & Waxman, S. (2013). Commentary on special section: Deficit or difference? Interpreting diverse Developmental Paths. *Developmental Psychology, 49,* 80–83. doi:10.1037/a0029741

Cole, M. (1996). *Cultural psychology: A once and future discipline.* Cambridge, MA: Harvard University Press.

Delgado-Gaitan, C. (1994). Socializing young children in Mexican-American families: An intergenerational perspective. In P. Greenfield & R. Cocking (Eds.),

Cross-cultural roots of minority child development (pp. 55–86). Hillsdale, NJ: Erlbaum.

Flores, Y. G., & Manzo, R. D. (2012). Preparing teachers to instruct Latino children in U.S. schools. *Teacher Education and Practice, 25*(4), 572–575.

Fuller, B., & Garcia Coll, C. (2010). Learning from Latinos: Contexts, families, and child development in motion. *Developmental Psychology, 46,* 559–565. doi:10.1037/a0019412.

Gauvain, M., Munroe, R., & Beebe, H. (2013). Children's questions in cross-cultural perspective: A four-culture study. *Journal of Cross-Cultural Psychology, 44,* 1148–1165. doi:10.1177/0022022113485430

González, N., Andrade, R., Civil, M., & Moll, L. (2001). Bridging funds of distributed knowledge: Creating zones of practices in mathematics. *Journal of Education for Students Placed at Risk, 6*(1), 115–132. doi: http://dx.doi.org/10.1207/S15327671ESPR0601-2_7

Gutiérrez, K., Baquedano-López, P., & Tejeda, C. (1999). Rethinking diversity: Hybridity and hybrid language practices in the third space. *Mind, Culture, and Activity, 6,* 286–303. doi:http://dx.doi.org/10.1080/10749039909524733

Gutiérrez, K. D., & Rogoff, B. (2003). Cultural ways of learning: Individual traits or repertoires of practice. *Educational Researcher, 32,* 19–25. doi:https://doi.org/10.3102/0013189X032005019

Haden, C., Jant, E., Hoffman, P., Marcus, M., Geddes, J., & Gaskins, S. (2014). Supporting family conversations and children's STEM learning in a children's museum. *Early Childhood Research Quarterly, 29,* 333–344. doi:10.1016/j.ecresq.2014.04.004

Hammer, D., & van Zee, E. (2006). *Seeing the science in children's thinking: Case studies of student inquiry in physical science.* Portsmouth, NH: Heinemann.

Hart, B., & Risley, T. (1995). *Meaningful differences in the everyday experience of young American children.* Baltimore, MD: Brookes.

Heath, S. B. (1983). *Ways with words: Language, life, and work in communities and classrooms.* Cambridge, England: Cambridge University Press.

Lee, C. (2006). 'Every good-bye ain't gone': Analyzing the cultural underpinnings of classroom talk. *International Journal of Qualitative Studies in Education, 19,* 305–327. doi:10.1080/09518390600696729

Lee, O., & Buxton, C. (2013). Integrating science and English proficiency for English language learners. *Theory into Practice, 52,* 36–42. doi:10.1080/0735 1690.2013.743772

Losey, K. M. (1995). Mexican American students and classroom interaction: An overview and critique. *Review of Educational Research, 65,* 283–318. doi:https://doi.org/10.3102/00346543065003283

Luce, M., Callanan, M., & Smilovic, S. (2013). Links between parents' epistemological stance and children's evidence talk. *Developmental Psychology, 49*(3), 454–461. doi:10.1037/a0031249

McIntyre, E., Rosebery, A., & Gonzalez, N. (2001) *Classroom diversity: Connecting curriculum to students' lives.* Portsmouth, NH: Heinemann.

Medin, D., Bennis, W., & Chandler, M. (2010). Culture and the home-field disadvantage. *Perspectives on Psychological Science, 5,* 708–713. doi:10.1177/1745691610388772

Michaels, S. (2005). Can the intellectual affordances of working-class storytelling be leveraged in school? *Human Development, 48*, 136–145. doi:10.1159/000085516

Miller, P. J., Cho, G. E., & Bracey, J. R. (2005). Working-class children's experience through the prism of personal storytelling. *Human Development, 48*, 115–135. doi:10.1159/000085515

Miller, P. J., & Sperry, D. (2012). Déjà vu: The continuing misrecognition of low-income children's verbal abilities. In S. Fiske & H. R. Markus (Eds.), *Facing social class: How societal rank influences interaction* (pp. 109–130). New York, NY: Russell Sage Foundation.

National Research Council. (2012). *A framework for K–12 science education: Practices, cross-cutting concepts, and core ideas.* Washington, DC: National Academies Press. doi:10.17226/13165

Portales, R., & Portales, M. (2005). *Quality education for Latinos and Latinas: Print and oral skills for all students K–college.* Austin, TX: University of Texas Press.

Rogoff, B. (2003). *The cultural nature of human development.* New York, NY: Oxford University Press.

Rogoff, B. (2014). Learning by observing and pitching in to family and community endeavors: An orientation. *Human Development, 57*, 69–81. doi:10.1159/000356757

Rowley, S. J., & Camacho, T. C. (2015). Increasing diversity in cognitive developmental research: Issues and solutions. *Journal of Cognition and Development, 16*, 683–692. doi:10.1080/15248372.2014.976224

Siegel, D., Esterly, J., Callanan, M., Wright, R., & Navarro, R. (2007). Conversations about science across activities in Mexican-descent families. *International Journal of Science Education, 29*, 1447–1466. doi:10.1080/09500690701494100

Solis, G., & Callanan, M. (2016). Evidence against deficit accounts: Conversations about science in Mexican heritage families living in the United States. *Mind, Culture, and Activity, 23*, 212–224. doi:10.1080/10749039.2016.1196493

Solis, G., & Callanan, M. (in press). Parental guidance during a science-related activity in Mexican-heritage families from two schooling groups. Manuscript submitted for publication.

Sperry, D. E., Sperry, L. L., & Miller, P. J. (2015). Language socialization. In K. Tracy, C. Ilie, & T. Sandel (Eds.), *The international encyclopedia of language and social interaction,* (Vol. II, pp. 1–17). Hoboken, NJ: Wiley-Blackwell. doi:10.1002/9781118611463.wbielsi114

Tenenbaum, H., & Callanan, M. A. (2008). Parents' science talk to their children in Mexican descent families residing in the U.S.A. *International Journal of Behavioral Development, 32*, 1–12. doi:10.1177/0165025407084046

Tizard, B., & Hughes, M. (1984). *Young children learning.* Cambridge, MA: Harvard University Press.

Valencia, R. R, & Solorzano, D. G. (1997). Contemporary deficit thinking. In R. R. Valencia (Ed.), *The evolution of deficit thinking: Educational thought and practice* (pp. 160–210). London, England: Falmer Press.

CHAPTER 4

CULTURALLY COMPETENT MATHEMATICS INSTRUCTION FOR AFRICAN AMERICAN CHILDREN

A Review of Promising Practices in Schools, Classrooms, Homes and Communities

Jeffrey Brown, Cassandra Schreiber, and Oscar Barbarin

The Academy Award-winning film, *Hidden Figures* (Gigliotti et al., 2016), presents an important yet often obscured part of American history: how three African American female pioneers calculated by hand the complex equations that allowed NASA astronauts to travel safely to space in the late 1960s. What *Hidden Figures* offers is a counternarrative to the prevailing flood of stories of African American students' failure in mathematical achievement. Building on this counterexample, the purpose of this chapter is to explore the unique challenges African American children face in mathematics education due to issues of discrimination, and to highlight the role of family engagement as a source of resilience that supports children and sets them on pathways to academic success. Specifically, this chapter

Promising Practices for Engaging Families in STEM Learning, pp. 49–61
Copyright © 2018 by Information Age Publishing

reviews promising practices for, and provides recommendations about, how school leaders, teachers, and families can work together to positively influence mathematical outcomes for African American children.

MATHEMATICS EDUCATION AND AFRICAN AMERICAN CHILDREN

Mathematical knowledge and skills are essential for children's academic, cognitive, and social development beginning in early childhood and continuing through college (Claesens & Engel, 2013; Doctoroff, Fisher, Burrows, & Edman, 2016). For example, mathematical skills are associated with general cognitive development and children who develop strong mathematical skills are more likely to succeed in social studies and science (e.g., Coleman, 2013; Fuchs et al., 2006). Moreover, mathematical achievement is linked to positive peer relationships and prosocial skills (Oberle & Schonert-Reichl, 2012).

Statistics show that there are significant differences in the mathematical achievement of African American students in comparison to their White, Latino, and Asian peers. For example, nationally, in 4th grade mathematics, while 65% of Asian and 51% of White students are considered at or above proficient, only 26% of Latino students and 19% of African American students are so ranked (National Assessment of Educational Progress, 2015). For many African American students these gaps begin early in the preschool years and persist across formal schooling (Iruka, Gardner-Neblett, Matthews, & Winn, 2014).

These group variations are firmly rooted in the historical, political, and institutional barriers that African American children face, including racism, discrimination, and poverty. Because of this, researchers, policymakers, and educators must consider how race is central to students' mathematical learning (Martin, 2009). This requires a shift in thinking. Mathematics is often viewed as a discipline, consisting of correct numbers, formulas, and algorithms that exist in a vacuum, without consideration of language, culture, and time (Civil, 2016). Mathematics is therefore sometimes equated with intelligence in our society—that there are abstract ideas and symbols that people either grasp, or do not. Consequently, mathematics is often used as a gatekeeper in schools and applied to sort those who succeed, and those who do not.

Researchers and educators from the "critical race" perspective challenge this neutral, value-free perspective of mathematics and explicitly call out the field for playing a role in reproducing racial inequalities in mathematics (Diversity in Mathematics Education Center for Learning and Teaching [DiME], 2007; Ladson-Billings, 2006; Martin, 2009). These educators call for teaching and instruction that help students construct positive mathematical identities that resist and challenge the prevailing negative messages that might otherwise become internalized (Moses & Cobb, 2001; Moses, Kamii, Swap, & Howard, 1989). For example, The Algebra Project links the learning of algebra to the historical struggle for civil rights for African Americans, and views the practice of mathematics as an act of social justice. Critical race educators also argue that there are many mathematical practices and identities that students bring to the classroom from their home and local communities. For instance, Civil and Khan (2001) showed how to harness children's and families' existing knowledge about gardening to foster mathematical concepts about measurement. Gutstein (2003) demonstrated better mathematical outcomes for children in a middle school classroom using a mathematics-integrated social justice curriculum. These nontraditional, and culturally responsive methods are effective, and should not be marginalized in mathematics classrooms where teachers often rely on traditional instruction and scripts, but rather raised up, recognized, and valued (Moll, Amanti, Neff, & González, 2005).

PROMOTING AFRICAN AMERICAN MATHEMATICAL ACHIEVEMENT IN SCHOOLS, CLASSROOMS, AND HOMES AND COMMUNITIES

Bronfenbrenner's (1977) ecological systems theory, which places the child at the center of several nested systems that interact with each other (e.g., the family, school, and community), serves as the guiding framework for the practices and recommendations in this section. The focus here is on the development of mathematics achievement in the home, classroom, and school environments—all of which are situated within broader community and sociopolitical contexts. The suggested practices and recommendations, therefore, are not singular efforts devoid of wider contexts, but rather are interrelated parts of a wider effort to support the child and family system across multiple settings.

The Role of School Leaders: Setting a Vision That Promotes Equitable Opportunities

To promote equitable opportunities for African American children to study and learn mathematics, school leaders must communicate a vision of education to students, educators, and families that promotes culturally competent and unbiased school-wide curriculum, pedagogy, and assessment. Culturally competent education means creating an environment in which student orientations, language, backgrounds, and ethnic identities are valued and used as conduits of teaching, learning, and assessment (Ladson-Billings, 2006). Antibias education aligns these pillars with the process of deconstructing racism in schools and society (Matias & Mackey, 2016).

Response to Intervention (RTI; e.g., Fuchs & Fuchs, 2006) is one such antibias and culturally competent framework for educators. The framework is comprised of three tiers of multisystemic, team-based supports that emphasize focused, differentiated instruction and progress monitoring: the first tier involves universal screening and general, classroom-wide interventions; the second tier involves more focused interventions such as small groups; and the third tier involves specialized, often individualized supports for the student (Schulte, 2016). When applied correctly, RTI reduces the chances of inaccurate placement in special education services, especially for marginalized populations (Hosp & Madyun, 2007). RTI has been shown to improve academic outcomes from kindergarten through high school, and increases later graduation rates (Powers, Hagans, & Miller, 2007).

The culturally competent application of RTI to mathematics for African American students requires ongoing monitoring of progress, clear communication with staff and families about children's current educational experiences and future goals and expanding stakeholders' conceptions of what mathematical competence means (DiME, 2007). School leaders must ensure that teachers and parents understand the role of RTI in the intervention process, including early screening for difficulties, structured support at all levels, and problem solving when difficulties in mathematical performance arise. It also means educators must focus on what students are actually doing and how their knowledge is growing, and be able to convey students' strengths and challenges to parents along with actionable steps to provide support. Finally, administrators must provide multiple and ongoing opportunities for teachers and families to connect with one another at times that parents are available and that do not conflict with work schedules.

The Role of Classroom Teachers: Implementing Culturally Competent and Antibias Pedagogy

Aligned with culturally competent and antibias approaches, teachers can promote the mathematical achievement of African American students within their classrooms in a variety of ways, including helping students to overcome stereotype threat, promoting communal learning, and connecting in- and out-of-school knowledge.

Overcoming stereotype threat. Evidence suggests that one barrier to long-term mathematical achievement in African American children is stereotype threat, the theory that those with less power, including some ethnic minorities and females, show worse performance in academic domains (including mathematics) when the identities that are associated with lower skills are made more salient. This poor performance is related to the anxiety associated with being reminded about negative racial/ethnic or gender stereotypes (Steele, 1997; Steele & Aronson, 1995). The effect of stereotype threat is to limit children's ability to perform in mathematics and thus, to limit achievement. Teachers can help students overcome stereotype threat in mathematics by: (1) engaging students in experiences that reshape their mathematical identities; (2) helping them see that making mistakes is a normal part of the learning process; (3) affirming their racial identifies (e.g., by referencing the *Hidden Figures* story); and (4) helping them use mathematics as a tool for change (Martin, 2009). This can be a slow, gradual process but one that teachers should emphasize, regardless of whether students have expressed explicit attitudes about mathematical ability being linked to their racial/ethnic or gender identity, or being an immutable characteristic.

Promoting communal learning. Communal learning—moving away from a classroom model that relies solely upon individual work—can also increase the efficacy of mathematics teaching for African American students. For example, fifth grade African American students showed greater improvement in a mathematical estimation task in a "communal learning" condition than in an "individual learning" condition (Hurley, Boykin, & Allen, 2005). Key features of communal learning environments include collaboration and cooperation to complete tasks, group rewards, and an emphasis on social relationships and classroom community as a primary motivator for completing a task. Teachers can implement evidence-based group contingencies such as the Good Behavior Game, which has been shown to teach students to cooperatively display prosocial behaviors to earn a previously determined reward (Pennington & McComas, 2017). In a small group working on mathematics, for example, multistep problems can be divided up such that each student in the group completes one step, then all students come together to collaboratively complete the problem.

An important component of communal learning might also be the formation of peer networks (Walker, 2006). This involves creating environments in which peer tutors and group work outside of the classroom to foster positive mathematical outcomes.

Connecting in- and out-of-school knowledge. Culturally responsive mathematics teaching also incorporates into the curriculum students' daily lives outside of the classroom. Recent research on the opportunity gap has demonstrated the benefits of centering schools and classrooms around students' needs and experiences (Friedlaender et al., 2014). For example, teachers can develop word problems that build on students' daily routines, like walking to school with siblings (Peterek & Lott Adams, 2009). Teachers can also invite families into their classrooms to share stories of how they use mathematics in their daily lives and in their professions. In addition, incorporating mathematics exercises throughout other subject areas, such as reading and social studies, whenever applicable can promote positive mathematical outcomes for African American children (Boykin, Tyler, Watkins-Lewis, & Kizzie, 2006). These subject areas foster significant cultural connections between the children and the materials, while continuing to develop underlying cognitive abilities, such as quantitative reasoning and fluid reasoning, which are also activated during these related tasks.

Another leverage point for supporting African American children's mathematical development is through teachers explicitly discussing mathematical concepts and principles throughout the school day (National Research Council, 2009). Arnold, Fisher, Doctoroff, and Dobbs (2002) found that this improved early mathematical performance and increased satisfaction from learning mathematics, in a sample that was approximately 40% African American. Based on these findings, preschool teachers might emphasize how simple mathematical concepts can be used in tasks such as circle time, and elementary school teachers can talk about mathematics during line-up and the transition to recess. Teachers can also communicate to families how they might be able to do this in their everyday lives.

The Role of Families: eXposing, eXplaining, and eXpanding

Families play an important role in promoting children's mathematical competencies at home and in the broader community. Barbarin (2010) describes three strategies that are applicable for supporting African American children's mathematical development: eXpose, eXplain, and eXpand.

eXpose: eXpose refers to parents engaging children in enrichment activities that supplement what is learned in school or more formal educational settings. For example, families of young children who know that their child is learning about measurement might talk explicitly about how to measure the correct amount of laundry detergent during chores. For older children, topics from homework can be integrated into daily routines and chores (Jackson & Remillard, 2005). Other studies have described and investigated the positive effect of broader home strategies to improve mathematical outcomes. These include modeling, reinforcement, general oversight, structural involvement, and engagement with tasks (Gutman, Sameroff, & Eccles, 2002; Hoover-Dempsey et al., 2001).

eXplain: eXplain refers to families' use of conversations to help children make sense of their experiences and enhance their understanding of how things work. For example, families might use "math talk," where children are asked to describe their mathematical thinking through open-ended questions (e.g., a mother asking her son to figure out how much milk to pour into a cake recipe that has been doubled). eXplain can also refer to families explaining to children issues of race, politics, and power. For example, to help counteract potential stereotype threat, families can talk with children about intelligence as something that can be changed, while attributing lack of academic achievement to environmental factors rather than internal, inherent ability (Good, Aronson, & Inzlicht, 2003). To combat differential treatment, adults can explicitly emphasize that poor performance or difficulty on a mathematical task can be temporary and due to external, environmental circumstances as opposed to stable, internal characteristics. This forms a part of positive racial socialization, which can in turn promote positive trajectories in mathematics and other academic areas (Neblett et al., 2008).

eXpand: eXpand refers to the practice of elaborating on a child's knowledge to advance more complex way of thinking. For young children, this might mean helping a child to count the number of blocks in a set correctly by moving each one to the side after counting it. Parents can also expand children's mathematical knowledge by engaging them in out-of-school opportunities to learn and practice mathematics, such as formal after-school settings or library tutoring programs (McGee & Spencer, 2015). Families can also model and talk about their own mathematical experiences and introduce students to role models in the community who use mathematics in their professions.

Holding high expectations for children's learning is another important way that African American parents can expand opportunities for children's mathematical learning and improve children's mathematical outcomes. African American parents that have higher academic expectations for their children and those who are more engaged with the child's school tend to have children with greater academic gains (Galindo & Sheldon, 2012). Hill and Craft (2003) found that, for African American participants, higher parental expectations and school involvement tended to improve children's mathematics performance along with their general academic competency. School-based involvement and believing children will go far in school was the most consistently positive predictor of early elementary school achievement (Sibley & Dearing, 2014). High expectations matter because they may decrease the differential treatment that can negatively influence motivation (Kurtz-Costes & Woods, 2017).

RECOMMENDATIONS

For Schools

- Conduct staff professional development on culturally competent mathematical practices in the classroom. This involves challenging any negative assumptions the staff may have about the performance and ability of African American students.
- Design a system for home-school communication and parent engagement. Create incentives for parents to become involved in the school community. Include opportunities that do not conflict with possible work schedules.
- Implement and closely monitor academic and social-emotional curriculum and materials for cultural relevance, racial socialization, integration with other aspects of the students' lives, and malleable approaches to learning.

For Teachers

- Engage in regular home-school communication, involving parents as much as possible in assisting their child with mathematical knowledge and skills, including telling parents how they can reinforce these competencies at home and how best to support their child's homework.
- Explicitly state to students that mathematical ability is highly malleable and not tied to characteristics such as gender or race. Specifically, discuss with them at an appropriate developmental level that their mathematical knowledge and skills will likely increase with further instruction and practice, and that parts of the difficulty are due to the novelty of the concept, rather than any innate skill deficits.
- Provide ample opportunities for students to work in teams and to collaborate with each other in the classroom. Emphasize the importance of mathematics as a part of the social learning community of the classroom by creating opportunities for mathematical knowledge and skills to be used throughout the daily routines of the classroom. In a kindergarten or prekindergarten classroom, this may include asking students to count how many other students there are during a station exercise or counting off students in a line during transitions.

For Parents

- Incorporate mathematics into daily chores, errands, and conversations around the house, asking the child to count, compute, or use mathematical reasoning, at an appropriate developmental level.
- Provide oversight for mathematics homework, both in terms of content supervision and the child's approach to the homework in general. Encourage a positive and resilient approach by rewarding effort and progress.
- Emphasize that mathematics and other academic abilities are characteristics that can change and develop over time. Refrain from discussing academic ability as a fixed, internal trait. Rather, ask the child to consider external reasons for why the task may be difficult, while exploring ways in which the child can maneuver through the difficulty. Explicitly socialize the child to believe that any problems that they may face are not due to race/ethnicity or other immutable characteristics.
- Maintain regular communication with the child's teacher and school, including asking to see progress monitoring tools for their in-classroom mathematics assessments and discussing techniques that can be employed at home to reinforce the particular mathematical concepts for the week, especially if there is little or no progress being made.

CONCLUSION

This chapter summarizes the best practices for promoting mathematical development in African American children. Schools, teachers, and families can employ these practices to best serve the instructional needs of these children, and to reduce academic and socioeconomic inequality. The chapter has conceptualized the African American child as being at the center of multiple systems of support. Thus, it is best to address mathematical instruction and intervention using this multi-systemic approach, fostering culturally competent RTI practices and classroom techniques, as well as parenting practices that involve engagement with the school and support at home. Beyond individual practices, parents and teachers need to instill positive racial socialization in response to the potential for stereotype threat to impact children's mathematical performance negatively. This strong foundation in mathematics will have far-reaching positive implications across academic, cognitive, and social domains.

REFERENCES

Arnold, D. H., Fisher, P. H., Doctoroff, G. L., & Dobbs, J. (2002). Accelerating mathematics development in Head Start classrooms. *Journal of Educational Psychology, 94*, 762–770. doi:10.1037/0022-0663.94.4.762

Barbarin, O. A. (2010). Halting African American boys' progression from pre-K to prison: What families, schools and communities can do! *American Journal of Orthopsychiatry, 80*(1), 81–88. doi:10.1111/j.1939-0025.2010.01009.x

Boykin, A. W., Tyler, K. M., Watkins-Lewis, K., & Kizzie, K. (2006). Culture in the sanctioned classroom practices of elementary school teachers serving low-income African American students. *Journal of Education for Students Placed at Risk, 11*(2), 161–173. doi:10.1207/s15327671espr1102_3

Bronfenbrenner, U. (1977). Toward an experimental ecology of human development. *American Psychologist, 32*(7), 513. doi:10.1037/0003-066X.32.7.513

Civil, M. (2016). STEM learning research through a funds of knowledge lens. *Cultural Studies of Science Education, 11*(1), 41–59. doi:10.1007/s11422-014-9648-2

Civil, M., & Khan, L. H. (2001). Mathematics instruction developed from a garden theme. *Teaching Children Mathematics, 7*(7), 400.

Claesens, A., & Engel, M. (2013). How important is where you start? Early mathematics knowledge and later school success. *Teachers College Record, 115*(6), 1–29. Retrieved from http://www.tcrecord.org/Content.asp?ContentId=16980

Coleman, B. (2013). Interdisciplinary strategies for math and social studies. In T. Linter (Ed.), *Integrative strategies for the K–12 social studies classroom* (pp. 103–126). Charlotte, NC: IAP Information Age Publishing.

Diversity in Mathematics Education Center for Learning and Teaching [DiME]. (2007). Culture, race, power, and mathematics education. In F. Lester (Ed.), *Second handbook of research on mathematics teaching and learning* (Vol. 1, pp. 405–433). Reston, VA: National Council of Teachers of Mathematics. doi:QA11. S365 2007 510.71-dc22

Doctoroff, G. L., Fisher, P. H., Burrows, B. M., & Edman, M. T. (2016). Preschool children's interest, social–emotional skills, and emergent mathematics skills. *Psychology in the Schools, 53*(4), 390–403. doi:http://dx.doi.org.ezproxy.mnsu.edu/10.1002/pits.21912

Friedlaender, D., Burns, D., Lewis-Charp, H., Cook-Harvey, C. M., Zheng, X., & Darling-Hammond, L. (2014). *Student-centered schools: Closing the opportunity gap*. Stanford, CA: Stanford Center for Opportunity Policy in Education. Retrieved from https://edpolicy.stanford.edu/sites/default/files/scope-pub-student-centered-cross-case.pdf

Fuchs, D., & Fuchs, L. S. (2006). Introduction to response to intervention: What, why, and how valid is it? *Reading Research Quarterly, 41*(1), 92–99. doi:10.1598/RRQ.41.1.4

Fuchs, L. S., Fuchs, D., Compton, D. L., Powell, S. R., Seethaler, P. M., ... Fletcher, J. M. (2006). The cognitive correlates of third-grade skill in arithmetic, algorithmic computation, and arithmetic word problems. *Journal of Educational Psychology, 98*(1), 29. doi:10.1037/0022-0663.98.1.29

Galindo, C., & Sheldon, S. B. (2012). School and home connections and children's kindergarten achievement gains: The mediating role of family involvement. *Early Childhood Research Quarterly, 27*(1), 90–103. doi:http://dx.doi.org.ezproxy.mnsu.edu/10.1016/j.ecresq.2011.05.004

Gigliotti, D., Chernin, P., Topping, J., Williams, P. & Melfi, T. (Producers) & Melfi, T. (Director). *Hidden Figures* [Motion picture]. United States: Fox 2000 Pictures, Chernin Entertainment & Levantine Films.

Good, C., Aronson, J., & Inzlicht, M. (2003). Improving adolescents' standardized test performance: An intervention to reduce the effects of stereotype threat. *Applied Developmental Psychology, 24*, 645–662. doi:10.1016/j.appdev.2003.09.002

Gutman, L. M., Sameroff, A. J., & Eccles, J. S. (2002). The academic achievement of African American students during early adolescence: An examination of multiple risk, promotive, and protective factors. *American Journal of Community Psychology, 30*(3), 367–400. doi:http://dx.doi.org.ezproxy.mnsu.edu/10.1023/A:1015389103911

Gutstein, E. (2003). Teaching and learning mathematics for social justice in an urban, Latino school. *Journal for Research in Mathematics Education, 34*(1), 37–73. doi:10.2307/30034699

Hill, N. E., & Craft, S. A. (2003). Parent-school involvement and school performance: Mediated pathways among socioeconomically comparable African American and Euro-American families. *Journal of Educational Psychology, 95*(1), 74–83. doi:http://dx.doi.org.ezproxy.mnsu.edu/10.1037/0022-0663.95.1.74

Hoover-Dempsey, K., Battiato, A. C., Walker, J. M. T., Reed, R. P., DeJong, J. M., & Jones, K. P. (2001). Parental involvement in homework. *Educational Psychologist, 36*(3), 195–209. doi:http://dx.doi.org.ezproxy.mnsu.edu/10.1207/S15326985EP3603_5

Hosp, J. L., & Madyun, N. H. (2007). Addressing disproportionality with response to intervention. In S. R. Jimerson, M. K. Burns, & A. M. VanDerHeyden (Eds.), *Handbook of response to intervention: The science and practice of assessment and intervention* (2nd ed., pp. 172–181). New York, NY: Springer Science + Business Media. doi:http://dx.doi.org.ezproxy.mnsu.edu/10.1007/978-0-387-49053-3_13

Hurley, E. A., Boykin, A. W., & Allen, B. A. (2005). Communal versus individual learning of a math-estimation task: African American children and the culture of learning contexts. *The Journal of Psychology: Interdisciplinary and Applied, 139*(6), 513–527. doi:http://dx.doi.org.ezproxy.mnsu.edu/10.3200/JRLP.139.6.513-528

Iruka, I. U., Gardner-Neblett, N., Matthews, J. S., & Winn, D. M. C. (2014). Preschool to kindergarten transition patterns for African American boys. *Early Childhood Research Quarterly, 29*, 106–117. doi:10.1016/j.ecresq.2013.11.004

Jackson, K., & Remillard, J. T. (2005). Rethinking parent involvement: African American mothers construct their roles in the mathematics education of their children. *The School Community Journal, 15*(1), 51–73. Retrieved from http://repository.upenn.edu/gse_pubs/11/

Kurtz-Costes, B. E., & Woods, T. A. (2017). Race and ethnicity in the study of competence motivation. In A. J. Elliot, C. S. Dweck, & D. S. Yaeger (Eds.),

Handbook of competence and motivation: Theory and application (2nd ed., pp. 529–546). New York, NY: Guilford.

Ladson-Billings, G. (2006). From the achievement gap to the education debt: Understanding achievement in U.S. schools. *Educational Researcher, 35*(7), 3–12.

Martin, D.B. (2009). Liberating the production of knowledge about African American children and mathematics. In D. Martin (Ed.), *Mathematics teaching, learning, and liberation in African American contexts* (pp. 3–36). London, England: Routledge. doi:10.1111/j.1548-1492.2010.01081.x

Matias, C. E., & Mackey, J. (2016). Breakin' down whiteness in antiracist teaching: Introducing critical whiteness pedagogy. *The Urban Review, 48*(1), 1–19. doi:10.1007/s11256-015-0344-7

McGee, E., & Spencer, M.B. (2015). Black parents as advocates, motivators, and teachers of mathematics. *The Journal of Negro Education, 84*(3), 473–490. doi:10.7709/jnegroeducation.84.3.0473

Moll, L., Amanti, C., Neff, D., & González, N. (Eds.). (2005). Funds of knowledge for teaching: Using a qualitative approach to connect homes and classrooms. In *Funds of knowledge: Theorizing practices in households, communities, and classrooms* (pp. 71–88). Mahwah, NJ: Lawrence Erlbaum Associates. doi:10.4324/9781410613462

Moses, R. P., & Cobb, C. E. (2001). *Radical equations: Math literacy and civil rights.* Boston, MA: Beacon Press.

Moses, R. P., Kamii, M., Swap, S. M., & Howard, J. (1989). The Algebra Project: Organizing in the spirit of Ella. *Harvard Educational Review, 59*(4), 423–443. Retrieved from: http://www.cpn.org/sections/topics/youth/stories-studies/algebra_project.html

National Assessment of Educational Progress. (2015). *The nation's report card-2015; 4th and 8th Grade mathematics assessments.* Retrieved from https://www.nationsreportcard.gov/reading_math_2015/#mathematics?grade=4

National Research Council. (2009). *Mathematics learning in early childhood: Paths toward excellence and equity.* Washington, DC: The National Academies Press. doi:https://doi.org/10.17226/12519

Neblett, E. W., White, R. L., Ford, K. R., Philip, C. L., Nguyen, H. X., & Sellers, R. M. (2008). Patterns of racial socialization and psychological adjustment: Can parental communications about race reduce the impact of racial discrimination? *Journal of Youth and Adolescence, 18*, 477–515. doi:10.1111/j.1532-7795.2008.00568.x

Oberle, E., & Schonert-Reichl, K. A. (2013). Relations among peer acceptance, inhibitory control, and math achievement in early adolescence. *Journal of Applied Developmental Psychology, 34*(1), 45–51. doi:10.1016/j.appdev.2012.09.003

Pennington, B., & McComas, J. J. (2017). Effects of the good behavior game across classroom contexts. *Journal of Applied Behavior Analysis, 50*(1), 176–180. doi:10.1002/jaba.357

Peterek, E., & Lott Adams, T. (2009). Meeting the challenge of engaging students for success in mathematics by using culturally responsive methods. In D. Y. White & J. S. Spitzer (Eds.), *Mathematics for every student: Responding to diversity, grades pre-K–5* (pp. 149–160). Reston, VA: The National Council of Teachers of Mathematics. Retrieved from https://www.nctm.org/store/Products/Mathe-matics-for-Every-Student,-Responding-to-Diversity,-Grades-PreK-5-(eBook)/

Powers, K., Hagans, K., & Miller, M. (2007). Using response to intervention to promote transition from special education services. In S. R. Jimerson, M. K. Burns, & A. M. VanDerHeyden (Eds.), *Handbook of response to intervention: The science and practice of assessment and intervention* (2nd ed., pp. 418–427). New York, NY: Springer Science + Business Media. doi:http://dx.doi.org.ezproxy.mnsu.edu/10.1007/978-0-387-49053-3_31

Schulte, A. C. (2016). Prevention and response to intervention: Past, present, and future. In S. R. Jimerson, M. K. Burns, & A. M. VanDerHeyden (Eds.), *Handbook of response to intervention: The science and practice of multi-tiered systems of support* (2nd ed., pp. 59–71). New York, NY: Springer Science + Business Media. doi:http://dx.doi.org.ezproxy.mnsu.edu/10.1007/978-1-4899-7568-3_5

Sibley, E., & Dearing, E. (2014). Family educational involvement and child achievement in early elementary school for American-born and immigrant families. *Psychology in the Schools, 51*(8), 814–831. doi:10.1002/pits.21784

Steele, C. M. (1997). A threat in the air: How stereotypes shape intellectual identity and performance. *American Psychologist, 52*(6), 613–629. doi:10.1037/0003-066X.52.6.613

Steele, C. M., & Aronson, J. (1995). Stereotype threat and the intellectual test performance of African Americans. *Journal of Personality and Social Psychology, 69*(5), 797–811. doi http://dx.doi.org.ezproxy.mnsu.edu/10.1037/0022-3514.69.5.797

Walker, E. (2006). Urban high school students' academic communities and their effects on mathematics success. *American Educational Research Journal, 43*(1), 43–73. doi:https://doi.org/10.3102/00028312043001043

SECTION II

MODELS AND APPROACHES TO
ENGAGING FAMILIES IN STEM

Section I laid out research-based ways that school and community educators can engage families in STEM learning and discussed how to democratize STEM education, particularly in the cases of Latino and African American families, and adults with math anxiety. In Section II, we build on this research by presenting four different approaches and program models to engaging families in STEM.

In Chapter 5, Duch and Gennetian explore the efficacy of a mathematics-focused intervention constructed with a behavioral economics approach. This approach acknowledges that families—especially those from low-income homes—are busy juggling day to day demands that can make decision making and engagement in children's learning difficult. However, low-cost program modifications can reverse this trend, especially among families who may be disenfranchised.

In Chapter 6, McWayne, Mistry, Brenneman, Zan, and Greenfield describe how the "funds of knowledge" approach can help early childhood educators incorporate immigrant families' rich cultural resources into science, technology, and engineering curricula. Through a longitudinal project to promote parent-teacher discussion groups and joint learning, the authors show how this approach to family-school-community partnerships is particularly powerful for dual language learners.

In Chapter 7, Chklovski and Jaris introduce collective impact approaches that recognize that no single organization can improve students' STEM achievement alone; but rather all parts of the STEM ecosystem must join together. They highlight how their program successfully brings students, families, educators, and engineers together—both virtually and in-person—to engage in design challenges and increase families' and students' knowledge, confidence, and attitudes about STEM.

Finally, in Chapter 8, Uscianowski, Almeda, and Ginsburg show how dialogic reading approaches—where parents actively engage with children during story sharing—can be extended to digital media. By focusing on one interactive mathematics storybook, the authors demonstrate how these digital tools can be used to foster family engagement in children's mathematical learning.

Collectively, this section demonstrates that, by working together and recognizing each other's expertise, educators and families can develop meaningful programs and curricula that motivate children to learn the STEM skills they need to succeed in today's technological and economic climate. The chapters also highlight how digital media and technology are not only an area to be studied and explored, but also an effective mechanism to reach and engage families.

CHAPTER 5

USING A BEHAVIORAL ECONOMICS PERSPECTIVE TO BOOST FAMILY ENGAGEMENT IN THE *GETTING READY FOR SCHOOL* PRESCHOOL INTERVENTION

Helena Duch and Lisa A. Gennetian

Alice is a coach for a 10-week parenting program that includes supplemental workshops and parties to demonstrate fun ways to interact with young children on math and reading; like all dedicated service providers, Alice takes outreach and recruitment seriously. She knows from her prior experience that getting parents to show up at least once early on is a stepping stone to further engagement. Alice combines her own successful experiences with the best-known strategies out there, including one-on-one phone calls and offering food and child care. Despite these best efforts, attendance is often disappointing and can be spotty. Some parents say they are interested, and some even say they will attend, but many times these same parents do not follow through.

Promising Practices for Engaging Families in STEM Learning, pp. 65–80
Copyright © 2018 by Information Age Publishing
All rights of reproduction in any form reserved.

The challenge Alice faces in engaging parents resonates for many dedicated service providers. The behavioral economics framework offers a new perspective—and a new set of tools—to engage parents in programs and educational opportunities to reduce these kinds of intention-to-action gaps, where parents fail to follow through, even with the best of intentions.

This chapter introduces concepts from behavioral economics as an approach to boost family engagement and describes an application of these concepts in preschoolers' mathematics for one specific program, *Getting Ready for School*. Described in more detail below, the interdisciplinary perspective of behavioral economics offers a complementary set of new tools that marshal and recognize how mental resources and contextual factors can influence—and thus interfere with—parents' decisions to participate and follow through with activities that are believed to support young children's development.

WHAT IS BEHAVIORAL ECONOMICS?

Behavioral economics is a blended theoretical perspective from economics, social psychology, and cognitive decision making, and views family engagement as the result of a series of small decisions that parents make and are encouraged to make repeatedly (Gennetian, Darling, & Aber, 2016). Behavioral economics views the brain not as a computer, but as a complex system that is influenced by other people's actions and opinions, with cognitive resources that can be enhanced or drained (loosely referred to here as "mental bandwidth"). Behavioral economics explicitly considers the ways in which parents' situations affect their decision making. This is especially important in the context of early childhood interventions, many of which are targeted to income-poor families who are struggling to make their finances meet basic day to day necessities; this juggling can further strain mental resources—such as attention—which are necessary to participate in intervention programs (Gennetian & Shafir, 2015; Mullainathan & Shafir, 2013).

Barriers such as these may be particularly heightened in the area of early math exposure (or STEM more generally), as public knowledge about its value during early childhood is relatively nascent and less normalized than early language or overall early brain development. Further, the fundamentals of math and the ways in which math are already used in day-to-day living are not well understood. Thus, parents often make false assumptions about math as complex theorizing, highly formulaic, or, worse, can typecast math as only being suitable for certain children with real or perceived inherent analytic capacity.

Many early interventions that support and promote family engagement in children's STEM or math development presume that once structural or personal barriers (like child care or transportation) have been addressed, parents are able and willing to respond, and will do so. The behavioral economic lens considers how parents' attention can be redirected toward program goals, understanding that they are busy juggling other demands; that their multiple identities as workers, friends, spouses, protectors, and nurturers may not equally align with program objectives; and that the ways in which other trusted parents and peers choose to act, and related social norms, can influence their decisions. Behavioral economics also considers the ways in which the context of decisions can influence choices. This has implications for the design of interventions; for example, choosing a desired default option when an active decision is *not* made can be leveraged to increase parents' engagement, as well as children's interactions and experiences (Thaler & Sunstein, 2008). Examples of several highly utilized design enhancements and tools that emerge from the behavioral economic lens are described in the Appendix of Gennetian, Darling, and Aber (2016).

FAMILY ENGAGEMENT AND MATH: WHY IT MATTERS

Disparities in academic achievement among U.S. children are already apparent in elementary school, suggesting the importance of the home and early school environment in the development of academic skills (Janus & Duku, 2007). The multitude of ways that parents and families interact with children during the years before formal schooling can be broadly understood as one component of family engagement that provides a foundation for subsequent school readiness and skill development (Van Voorhis, Maier, Epstein, & Lloyd, 2013). Although there is a strong evidence base for the role of family engagement in literacy development, recent studies also point to the influence of math development during these early years as an additional significant predictor of future socioemotional and academic outcomes (Duncan et al., 2007; Huntsinger, Jose, & Luo, 2016).

Early math skills do not develop in isolation; they grow with language and social skills, and require support from parents and other family members. Although parents are more likely to engage in literacy activities on a weekly basis with their children, as little as one math related activity a week can have significant implications for children's development (Berkowitz et al., 2015; LeFevre et al., 2009). Many factors inform the level of family engagement in math with their children, including parental education, parental math anxiety, cultural norms, mindsets and attitudes about math development, and access to a math-rich home environment, which includes easy access to children's books, puzzles, and blocks (Berkowitz et al., 2015; Cankaya & LeFevre, 2016; LeFevre et al., 2009; Ma, Shen, Krenn, Hu, & Yuan, 2016; Skwarchuk, 2009). A growing base of evidence also suggests the importance of indirect math learning opportunities, which parents often do not consider "math," such as reading a book that includes math language, or sharing experiences such as cooking or shopping during which children can practice basic math skills (Bradley & Corwyn, 2016).

USING BEHAVIORAL ECONOMICS TO IMPROVE FAMILY ENGAGEMENT

Parents play a pivotal role in the development of math skills in preschool aged children, making this a critical point at which to intervene and conduct further research. Behavioral economics offers a framework for helping practitioners like Alice understand and creatively design approaches to address the obstacles parents tell us interfere with their engagement in supplemental programs, including math and STEM. Best practices available to family engagement program developers from conventional frameworks often point to educational workshops, brochures/pamphlets, and related digital formats as outreach and implementation strategies to share information and encourage parent buy-in and participation. In addition to not recognizing the challenges related to mental bandwidth, these strategies are often not rooted in, or expanded from, the math-related activities parents may already be doing with their children, nor designed in ways to pinpoint anxieties (see Chapter 2 in this volume). The following quotes from parents, and strategies to address them, illustrate how behavioral economics can offer new strategies for parent engagement:

"They told me about this meeting, and I totally forgot about it." Although conventional frameworks might suggest that more information alone will matter (e.g., more brochures in children's backpacks), the behavioral economics lens points us to the role of limited attention and distractions and suggests the value of more targeted and personalized reminders.

"He loses interest very fast with numbers." "I don't see him advance. Like I see him a little bit more into play than learning." By incorporating the child's perspective, giving feedback to parents that playing is learning, or re-crafting the rewards such that benefits are accrued today (vs. the ambiguous future), the behavioral economic lens offers new tools to help shift parents' fixed mindsets and inaccurate assumptions.

"When I first began I was like, 'I can't do this game. I'm not doing this.'" Whereas other frameworks might suggest education to alter parents' attitudes, behavioral economics suggests that one strategy to overcome low

parent confidence is to incorporate positive affirmations of parents as capable "teachers."

GETTING READY FOR SCHOOL: A UNIQUE APPROACH TO ENGAGING PARENTS IN PRESCHOOLERS' MATH LEARNING

Getting Ready for School (GRS) is a preschool intervention that integrates early math, literacy, and self-regulation skills into a single add-on intervention that can supplement curricula already implemented in preschool classrooms. At the heart of GRS is a strong belief in the power of parents and teachers working together to provide foundational experiences in emergent math, literacy, and self-regulation skills. Both the home and preschool environments independently influence child development (Andersson, Sommerfelt, Sonnanderm & Ahlsten, 1996), thus both environments must be supported. In fact, multipronged interventions targeting parents, teachers, or both often find a joint approach to be most efficacious (Beauchaine, Webster-Stratton, & Reid, 2005; Whitehurst et al., 1994).

The home component of GRS has developed into a matrix of services that allows families to engage with the intervention in distinct ways:

1. **Parent activity book.** At the core of GRS is a parent activity book, with nine units that mirror the classroom units. Activities are meant to be integrated into family life, for example going on a number hunt while out for a community walk, or forming pattern sequences with objects found in the home. They are designed to be fun ways for parents and children to interact and simultaneously encourage the development of early learning skills and knowledge.
2. **Weekly teacher-parent letters.** On a weekly basis, teachers complete a home/school connection letter that lets parents know about the kinds of activities and skills that children are learning at school and directs them to suggested activities in the parent book that may reinforce those activities in the home.
3. **Parent workshops.** Eight workshops are offered throughout the academic year. Workshops are interactive and offer parents or other caregivers the opportunity to learn basic concepts about the development of early math, literacy and self-regulation skills, practice activities and share experiences with other families.
4. **GRS Parties.** Parties take place during pick up time in the classroom and invite parents and children to interact with the materials and receive tips and coaching from teachers. In addition, parties provide food and raffles for books and toys.

5. **Digital and social media.** GRS offers families several ways to engage with program materials digitally. A program website includes videos of each of the activities in Spanish and English for families who want specific demonstrations on implementation. The videos are also available through tablets that are on loan in the classroom and can be checked out and brought home. Families are invited to join private Facebook groups where materials and activities specific to each classroom are shared.

BOOSTING FAMILY ENGAGEMENT IN GRS WITH BEHAVIORAL ECONOMIC ENHANCEMENTS

Although GRS set up these myriad programmatic options to reach out to families, similar to other early childhood programs, uptake was uneven, with little evidence that the program was reaching those families who could benefit the most. Simultaneously, data from the program demonstrated that increased family engagement yielded more growth in school readiness skills for the children (Marti, Xu, Repka, Gennetian, Kennedy, & Duch, 2017). With this in mind, and, with a strong desire to reach more families, the program set up a partnership to assess how family engagement could improve by applying insights from the field of behavioral economics. Engaging parents in the types of math activities such as those developed in GRS can be particularly challenging. Our preliminary analysis suggested that GRS workshops on the topics of children's self-regulation and literacy drew the highest attendance rates, while workshops on math had the lowest attendance rates.

To understand the types of decision-making and mental bandwidth barriers that might be getting in the way of family engagement, including family engagement in math, we first gathered information from parents about the actual GRS experience on the ground, from interviewing families in focus groups to surveys. This helped us to develop a few hypotheses about ways to integrate new types of designs and strategies into the existing GRS delivery process, described above. In 2015–2016, we implemented a bundle of behavioral economic enhancements with a random subset of families with children who attended Head Start programs in New York City, and who were receiving GRS (summarized in Table 5.1). The majority of the families in our study were Hispanic, had a high school degree or GED, and about one third were employed full-time at the beginning of the school year. The bundle of behavioral economic enhancements included:

- **A personalized written invitation to the kick-off meeting rather than the generic letter-sized flyer that had typically been used.** To convey some social proof, or external importance, of the event from a trusted source, the invitation explicitly mentioned that the child's teacher would also be in attendance; and, to prime parents' identity as not only their children's nurturer but also their first teacher, the invitation included a GRS branded image with the latter message (Allcott, 2011; Allcott & Mullainathan, 2010; Goldstein, Cialdini, & Greskevicius, 2008). To prompt parents to focus more attention on the personalized message, the postcard-sized invitation also included handwritten information about the location and time of the meeting (see postcard in Figure 5.1).

Figure 5.1.   Personalized invitation.

- **Commitment reminder via text to facilitate the translation of parents' intention to attend the kick-off meeting into action.** We asked parents to reply "Y" if they planned to attend the event (see Figure 5.2 for example text).

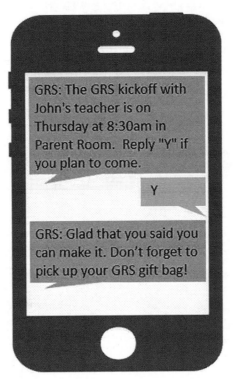

Figure 5.2.   Example of text based commitment.

- **Activity trackers instead of typical letters home from teachers to support the objective of increasing time spent on GRS activities outside of the classroom.** The activity trackers not only reinforced the fun nature of GRS activities—discarding the sense of homework-like responsibility conveyed by the previous letters—but also encouraged repeated parent-child engagement throughout the week (see Figure 5.3 for activity tracker).

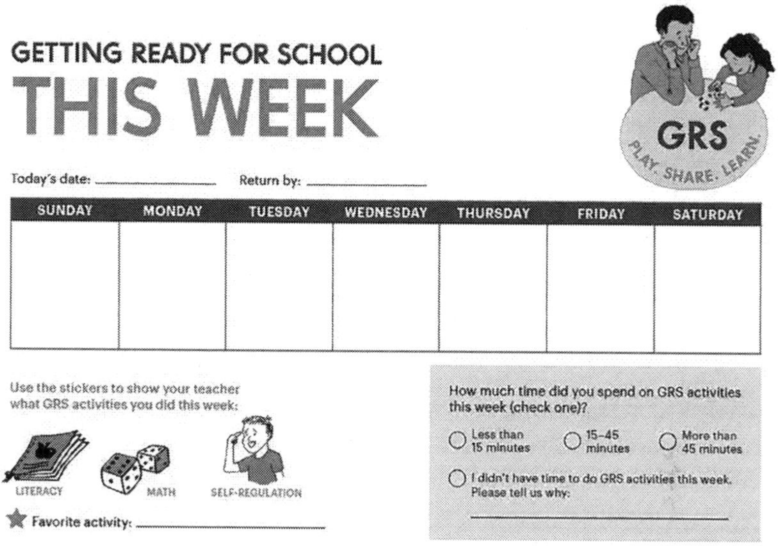

GETTING READY FOR SCHOOL

THIS WEEK

Today's date: _____   Return by: _____

SUNDAY	MONDAY	TUESDAY	WEDNESDAY	THURSDAY	FRIDAY	SATURDAY

Use the stickers to show your teacher
what GRS activities you did this week:

LITERACY   MATH   SELF-REGULATION

⭐ Favorite activity: _____

How much time did you spend on GRS activities
this week (check one)?

◯ Less than 15 minutes   ◯ 15–45 minutes   ◯ More than 45 minutes

◯ I didn't have time to do GRS activities this week.
Please tell us why:
_____

Figure 5.3.   Activity tracker.

Analyses showed consistent favorable impacts on family engagement as a result of this bundle of BE enhancements. Parents in the behavioral enhancement group were more likely to attend the beginning-of-year kick-off meeting; on average, returned twice as many activity trackers to their child's teacher; and spent a half hour more per week on GRS activities at home. The findings are particularly exciting as they suggest change not only in parents' in-the-moment decisions, but also cascading effects on parenting habits: parents in the behavioral enhancement group were more likely to attend GRS workshops without any additional reinforcement, and were more likely to return activity trackers multiple times.

BOOSTING FAMILY ENGAGEMENT IN GRS MATH WITH BEHAVIORAL ECONOMICS

With the 2015–2016 cohort data, we also learned that while family engagement appeared favorably related to children's literacy and behavioral outcomes, there was a less clear relation to math outcomes. This made us wonder if behavioral economic approaches could also encourage higher engagement of parents in the math-related programming and math activities of GRS. We drew from existing research about math and math engagement and intersected this with what we had already learned about the ways in which parents' mental bandwidth interacted with engagement in GRS more generally. Anxiety over math (computational) ability is high for much of the general population, including mothers (Ashcraft, 2002; Ashcraft & Ridley, 2005). Parents struggle with connecting math to everyday experiences, and lack goals and knowledge (Canon & Ginsberg, 2008). Such concerns are further fueled by misconceptions by preschool teachers about the appropriateness of teaching math to young children, beliefs among preschool teachers that children are "born" with innate math ability, and that language and literacy are more important than math (Lee & Ginsburg, 2009).

The 2016–2017 behavioral economic enhancements aimed to normalize math by interweaving fundamental math components appropriate for young children's development into day-to-day tasks and activities, and to empower parents about their capacity to teach and share in math-based tasks with their young children. In practice, this translated into text-based content pushed out to parents with personalized, targeted messages that incorporated a math concept (e.g., "more/less" to normalize math terms for parents) with a math-based task. For example:

- (More/less) Ask Lee which is more-2 big plates or 3 spoons. Not the plates, even though they're big. Math is a part of your everyday life.
- (Sort & compare) Ask Lee to sort the coins in your pocket. Are there more of any kind? Math is a part of your everyday life.

Some messages additionally included an image that visually conveyed a math concept in a usable, friendly manner such as:

- (Reading numbers) On the subway? Ask Lee to find 1, 2, 3, 4 and 5 in subway ads. Math is a part of your everyday life (see Figure 5.4).

Figure 5.4. Visual image to support families in reading numbers.

- (Measurement) Have Lee put objects (a spoon, crayon, and toothbrush) in order from little to big. Math is a part of your everyday life (see Figure 5.5).

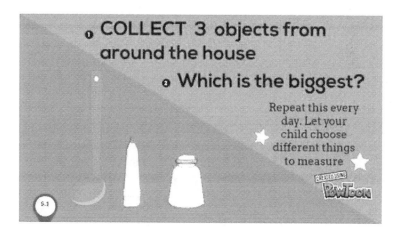

Figure 5.5. Visual image to support families in talking about measurement.

Finally, borrowing on the success of the personalized invitations tested in the prior year, we designed a personalized invitation to the GRS math workshop, emphasizing the variety of math concepts (e.g., "Shapes, numbers, patterns are all math") and the importance of math for future success (e.g., "Math today is a stepping stone to your child's success.")

We are still learning about the effectiveness of these approaches and impacts on parents' time spent with their children on GRS math activities with the 2016–2017 cohort of Head Start children. However, our preliminary analyses suggest that these behavioral economic enhancements had favorable influences on parent attendance at math workshops.

Table 5.1.
Description of GRS Outreach and Implementation Components and Behavioral Economic Enhancements

	GRS as usual	GRS with behavioral economic enhancements
Orientation	Black and white paper flyer	Personalized, handwritten colorful postcard
Reminders	One text prior to the workshop	Weekly reminders incorporated with weekly texts about GRS curriculum content
Weekly communication between teachers and parents	Teacher letter	Simplified teacher letter with child-friendly activity chart

LESSONS LEARNED: BOOSTING FAMILY ENGAGEMENT WITH TOOLS FROM BEHAVIORAL ECONOMICS

Our work using behavioral economics in GRS has provided many useful lessons that may help other programs as they consider how to better reach and engage families in their young children's learning, particularly around the area of math. Below we outline and summarize a few of these lessons:

- **Start with a good diagnostic process.** Surveys and focus groups with families helped us understand their needs and motivations, which allowed us to identify bottlenecks that go beyond the usual structural barriers, such as transportation and lack of time. Infusing a behavioral economics lens and thinking about issues of mental bandwidth, program uptake, and maintenance can be very useful in identifying new ways to support engagement with your program.

- **Offer a range of ways for families to engage with schools.** In any given program, families are heterogeneous, so it is unlikely that one family engagement modality will work for all. When we started our work with GRS, we used more typical family engagement activities, such as workshops and letters/fliers for parents. As we learned more about program families, we expanded our program to reflect their diversity.

- **Move away from attendance into sustained ways to support and measure engagement at home.** As we discussed above, schools and programs often shortchange themselves by narrowly defining involvement as a set of discrete events that parents do or do not attend. Instead, at GRS, we moved into a more sustainable way of figuring out how families spend time together supporting their children's learning, and how we can capture these interactions through activity trackers. We have broadened our view of engagement to ensure that we measure and track other ways in which teachers support parents and parents support children.

- **Design tailored solutions that are easy to implement and scale up.** The tools from behavioral economics offer small, low cost nudges that can help programs move the needle toward success. These nudges are typically small, easy to implement, can be streamlined into existing program practices, relatively low cost, and will contribute towards increased engagement and participation. A robust program is essential, but behavioral economics can help support your efforts and expand the reach of the program, sustainably, to families who might benefit the most.

- **Emphasize attendance at a gateway event.** At GRS, we realized that the kick-off event provided program orientation and was thus a gateway to all other activities. If parents attended that kick-off event, they learned about what was coming next in the year and how they could support their children's development. As a result, we place strong emphasis on increasing attendance to the kick-off. We suspect orientation is a key event for many schools and believe some of the behavioral economics strategies we used (personalization, priming of parents as first teachers) may help others boost participation.

- **Personalize your communication with parents.** Personalized invitations, content and outreach via text messages, and Facebook (and comparable digital or social media approaches) have yielded significant improvements in our family engagement efforts. Although personalization may seem burdensome, it is feasible to implement at scale with the many text-based and social media platforms that have mail-merging types of features. There is a one-time effort at the start of the year to enter everyone's information into a dataset, but once that information is available, it can be used across platforms and can have a sizable impact on family engagement.

The behavioral economics framework offers a new perspective and a new set of tools to improve parents' engagement in math and other programming. By attending to the contextual factors that might impact mental bandwidth—even among parents who are motivated to act—educators can ensure better access to their programming by the parents who need it most.

REFERENCES

Allcott, H. (2011). Social norms and energy conservation. *Journal of Public Economics, 95*(9-10), 1082–1095. doi:https://doi.org/10.1016/j.jpubeco.2011.03.003

Allcott, H., & Mullainathan, S. (2010). Behavior and energy policy. *Science, 327*(5970), 1204–1205. doi:10.1126/science.1180775

Andersson, H. W., Sommerfelt, K., Sonnander, K., & Ahlsten, G. (1996). Maternal child-rearing attitudes, IQ, and socioeconomic status as related to cognitive abilities of five-year-old children. *Psychological Reports, 79*(1), 3–14. doi:10.2466/pr0.1996.79.1.3

Ashcraft, M. H. (2002). Math anxiety: Personal, educational, and cognitive consequences. *Current Directions in Psychological Science, 11*(5), 181–185. doi:https://doi.org/10.1111/1467-8721.00196

Ashcraft, M. H., & Ridley, K. S. (2005). Math anxiety and its cognitive consequences: A tutorial review. In J. I. D. Campbell (Ed.), *Handbook of mathematical cognition* (pp. 315–327). New York, NY: Psychology Press.

Beauchaine, T. P., Webster-Stratton, C., & Reid, M. J. (2005). Mediators, moderators, and predictors of 1-year outcomes among children treated for early-onset conduct problems: A latent growth curve analysis. *Journal of Consulting and Clinical Psychology, 73*(3), 371–388. doi:10.1037/0022-006X.73.3.371

Berkowitz, T., Schaeffer, M. W., Maloney, E. A., Peterson, L., Gregor, C., Levine, S. C., & Beilock, S. L. (2015). Math at home adds up to achievement in school. *Science, 350*(6257), 196–198. doi:10.1126/science.aac7427

Bradley, R. H., & Corwyn, R. F. (2016). Home life and the development of competence in mathematics: Implications of research with the home inventory. In B. Blevins-Knabe & A. M. B. Austin (Eds.), *Early childhood mathematics skill development in the home environment* (pp. 29–49). Cham, Switzerland: Springer International.

Cankaya, O., & LeFevre, J.-A. (2016). The home numeracy environment: What do cross-cultural comparisons tell us about how to scaffold young children's mathematical skills? In B. Blevins-Knabe & A. M. B. Austin (Eds.), *Early childhood mathematics skill development in the home environment* (pp. 87–104). Cham, Switzerland: Springer International.

Canon, J., & Ginsberg, H. (2008). Doing the math: Maternal beliefs about early mathematics versus language learning. *Early Education and Development*, *19*(2), 238–260. doi:http://dx.doi.org/10.1080/10409280801963913

Duncan, G. J., Dowsett, C. J., Claessens, A., Magnuson, K., Huston, A. C., Klebanov, P. ... Brooks-Gunn, J. (2007). School readiness and later achievement. *Developmental Psychology*, *43*(6), 1428–1446. doi:10.1037/0012-1649.43.6.1428

Gennetian, L., Darling, M., & Aber, J. L. (2016). Behavioral economics and developmental science: A new framework to support early childhood interventions. *Journal of Applied Research on Children: Informing Policy for Children at Risk*, *7*(2). Retrieved from http://digitalcommons.library.tmc.edu/childrenatrisk/vol7/iss2/2/

Gennetian, L., & Shafir, E. (2015). The persistence of poverty in the context of financial instability: A behavioral perspective. *Journal of Policy Analysis and Management*, *34*(4), 904–936. doi:10.1002/pam.21854

Goldstein, N., Cialdini, R., & Griskevicius, V. (2008). A room with a viewpoint: Using social norms to motivate environmental conservation in hotels. *Journal of Consumer Research*, *35*(3), 472–482. doi:10.1086/586910

Huntsinger, C. S., Jose, P. E., & Luo, Z. (2016). Parental facilitation of early mathematics and reading skills and knowledge through encouragement of home-based activities. *Early Childhood Research Quarterly*, *37*, 1–15. doi:http://doi.org/10.1016/j.ecresq.2016.02.005

Janus, M., & Duku, E. (2007). The school entry gap: Socioeconomic, family, and health factors associated with children's school readiness to learn. *Early education and development*, *18*(3), 375–403.

LeFevre, J.-A., Skwarchuk, S.-L., Smith-Chant, B. L., Fast, L., Kamawar, D., & Bisanz, J. (2009). Home numeracy experiences and children's math performance in the early school years. *Canadian Journal of Behavioural Science/Revue canadienne des sciences du comportement*, *41*(2), 55–66. doi:http://dx.doi.org/10.1037/a0014532

Ma, X., Shen, J., Krenn, H. Y., Hu, S., & Yuan, J. (2016). A meta-analysis of the relationship between learning outcomes and parental involvement during early childhood education and early elementary education. *Educational Psychology Review*, *28*(4), 771–801. doi:https://doi.org/10.1007/s10648-015-9351-1

Marti, M., Xu, K., Repka, K., Gennetian, L., Kennedy, J., & Duch, H. (April, 2017). *A multi-dimensional approach to family engagement. Results from an integrated school readiness intervention.* Paper presented at the Society for Research on Child Development, Austin, TX.

Mullainathan, S., & Shafir, E. (2013). *Scarcity: Why having too little means so much.* New York, NY: Times Books.

Skwarchuk, S.-L. (2009). How do parents support preschoolers' numeracy learning experiences at home? *Early Childhood Education Journal*, *37*(3), 189–197. doi:https://doi.org/10.1007/s10643-009-0340-1

Lee, J. S., & Ginsberg, H. (2009). Early childhood teachers misconceptions about mathematics education for young children in the United States. *Australasian Journal of Early Childhood*, *34*(4), 37-45. Retrieved from https://earlyyearsliteracymath.wikispaces.com/file/view/Math+Reading.pdf

Thaler, R. H., & Sunstein, C. R. (2008). *Nudge: Improving decisions about health, wealth, and happiness*. New Haven, CT: Yale University Press.

Van Voorhis, F. L., Maier, M. F., Epstein, J. L., & Lloyd, C. M. (2013, October). The impact of family involvement on the education of children ages 3 to 8: A focus on literacy and math achievement outcomes and social-emotional skills. *MDRC*. Retrieved from https://www.mdrc.org/publication/impact-family-involvement-education-children-ages-3-8

Whitehurst, G. J., Arnold, D. S., Epstein, J. N., Angell, A. L., Smith, M., & Fischel, J. E. (1994). A picture book reading intervention in day care and home for children from low income families. *Developmental Psychology, 30*(5), 679–689.

CHAPTER 6

SUPPORTING FAMILY ENGAGEMENT IN SCIENCE, TECHNOLOGY, AND ENGINEERING (STE)[1] CURRICULUM AMONG LOW-INCOME IMMIGRANT FAMILIES WITH PRESCHOOL CHILDREN

Christine M. McWayne, Jayanthi Mistry,
Kimberly Brenneman, Betty Zan, and Daryl Greenfield

In the United States, disparities in achievement and opportunity linked to race/ethnicity, income, and home language are evident as early as the preschool years (APA Presidential Task Force on Educational Disparities, 2012; Espinosa, Laffey, & Whittaker, 2006). Awareness that the well-being of our nation is directly tied to the well-being of all individuals, especially our youngest generation, has led to a flood of mandates aimed at closing these gaps (e.g., *Every Student Succeeds Act*; Civic Impulse, 2017). In response to these mandates, a significant amount of research has aimed to identify protective factors against early risks that threaten later child outcomes. Family engagement (i.e., the multiple ways parents support their children's learn-

Promising Practices for Engaging Families in STEM Learning, pp. 81–97
Copyright © 2018 by Information Age Publishing

ing across multiple settings) and strong family-school connections have been identified as key protective factors for children's development and academic success (e.g., Ginsburg-Block, Manz, & McWayne, 2010). Thus, there is a growing sense of urgency around "getting families engaged" in children's education as early as possible (McWayne, 2015).

Yet, we lack adequate understanding of how to foster strong family-school partnerships, most notably demonstrated by poor evidence of success with existing family engagement programs (Mattingly, Prislin, McKenzie, Rodriguez, & Kayzar, 2002). A common narrative describes families who do not fit traditional expectations of involvement as "difficult" or "hard to reach." These families often come from cultural, linguistic, and/or socioeconomic backgrounds that are different from the mainstream educator. Thus, although agreeing that family-school partnerships are important, many educators can "harbor beliefs, attitudes, and fears about families that hinder their ability to cultivate partnerships" (Mapp & Hong, 2010, p. 346). And, although as educators we might not be aware of the implicit biases we hold, these realities foster disconnection and disengagement between families and education programs (Ramirez, 2003).

For immigrant families, in particular, the early years are a critical time to encourage family-school connections. By 2030, almost half of all school-aged children will be classified as English-language learners (ELLs; Thomas & Collier, 2002), with the highest concentrations in pre-K to third grade (Matthews & Ewen, 2006). During this period of early childhood, we refer to these children as "dual language learners," or DLLs, to acknowledge language development in both the home language and English. Gaps in learning and achievement between DLLs and their monolingual English-speaking peers appear as early as preschool (Park & McHuge, 2014; Reardon & Galindo, 2009). Because preschool is often the first contact between immigrant families and the formal U.S. education system, programs need to capitalize on this first contact with DLLs' families to support children's learning.

However, sociocultural differences between immigrant families and educators often translate into discontinuities between home and school. Differences between caregivers' and educators' values, socialization goals, beliefs about the specific role of parents and teachers in a child's education, and communication expectations and styles can place young children at risk for difficulties as they traverse these two settings. In addition, immigrant families' fears of government intervention and/or deportation often limit their willingness to engage with formal systems. Nevertheless, immigrant families care deeply about their children's education and have likely moved to the U.S. seeking employment and educational opportunities and a better life for their children.

We need new ways of thinking about family engagement that *begin* with trying to understand more about how to connect with families of DLLs (Delgado-Gaitan, 1991; Ramirez, 2003). In particular, the field needs to move beyond superficial ways of incorporating families' culture into the classroom (e.g., the "tourism" approach; Pattnaik, 2003) to develop more impactful ways to honor families in the formal curriculum (Civil & Andrade, 2003). By doing so, we honor children's familiar knowledge and affirm its relevance for their learning in school.

WHY IS STE A POTENTIALLY POWERFUL AREA OF EARLY CHILDHOOD CURRICULUM FOR DLLs AND FOR FOSTERING FAMILY-SCHOOL CONNECTIONS?

Young children have an innate motivation to explore the world and figure out how it works. Their curiosity includes both the natural world (science) and the human-made world (technology). Children design, or engineer, ways to make interesting things happen and create tools and methods (technologies) to solve problems. Although young children "may lack deep knowledge and extensive experience, they often engage in a wide range of subtle and complex reasoning about the world ... that can be used as a foundation to build *remarkable* [emphasis added] understanding" (National Research Council, 2012, pp. 24–25). Adults honor children by nurturing their natural curiosity and exploration, not just because it supports school readiness, but because it shows children that their interests matter. Early childhood teachers certainly are aware of young children's capacity for investigating and problem solving. What teachers may lack confidence in is knowing how to best support and scaffold children's inquiry, and how to capitalize on the many opportunities for STE learning that occur within the classroom and daily home lives of children.

STE represents a particularly ripe area of learning for DLLs, because strong STE pedagogy involves engaging children immediately with interesting materials, and with each other, in ways that invite exploration, inspire ideas, and provide ample opportunities to build skills across all domains of learning and development. STE learning can activate interest and promote learning across multiple domains, including bolstering children's executive functioning skills, their approaches to learning, collaboration with peers, mathematics understanding, and language development (Bustamante, White, & Greenfield, 2016; French, 2004; Gelman & Brenneman, 2011; Gelman, Brenneman, Macdonald, & Roman, 2009; Nayfeld, Fuccillo, & Greenfield, 2013).

We are particularly concerned about providing these experiences to DLL children, who often miss learning opportunities in which their curiosity about the natural and human-made world could be leveraged for future success. Unfortunately, stereotypes that squelch children's innate creativity and exploration begin early and can shut students out of the innovation pipeline (National Science Board, 2009). Educational equity demands that we create rich STE learning experiences for DLLs. Yet, for DLL children, access to engaging STE curriculum may be hampered not only by the well-documented barriers teachers experience to teaching STE (Greenfield et al., 2009), but also by a lack of connection to children's prior knowledge and cultural and community contexts. Families' work, hobbies, and everyday activities and routines serve as rich sources for building STE learning experiences (Moll, Amanti, Neff, & González, 2005). Engaging families in a process of *curriculum co-construction*—in which families and educators partner and collaborate with one another in mutually respectful and trusting ways—has the potential to create rich curricula that honor and incorporate the lived experiences of DLL children. These meaningful opportunities also address barriers to family engagement that many parents experience when mainstream expectations for parental involvement (e.g., volunteering in the classroom, reading to one's child) are the only options offered (Doucet, 2011; Hill, 2010).

THE RISE PROJECT[2]

We use our RISE (Readiness Through Integrative Science and Engineering) project (http://rise.as.tufts.edu) as an illustration of one approach to developing and implementing a STE curriculum that builds on both teachers' and families' existing practices and fosters home-school connections. Before delving into the specific home-school collaboration activities (the focus of this chapter), we provide here a bit of context for the overall RISE approach. Unlike a prescriptive (scripted) curriculum, co-construction of the RISE curriculum by families and educators is guided by a set of core principles (see Table 6.1).

In Figure 6.1, we illustrate how we initially developed key components of the RISE approach guided by these core principles. The top third of the figure emphasizes our commitment to building on existing strengths and experiential knowledge in classrooms, homes, and communities. We gathered information about teachers' STE practices from multiple sources including classroom observations, teachers' lesson plans and self-reports, and the classroom coach's observations. We gathered information about children's homes and communities through discussions with parents, neighborhood walks, and home observations. These sources of information helped us gain a better sense of what current practices and resources could be leveraged within the RISE curriculum, and to identify powerful "hooks" to engage children in STE learning of which teachers and parents might not be aware.

Table 6.1.

Core Principles of the RISE Approach to Early Childhood STE Curriculum and Professional Development

1. *Engage Diverse Perspectives and Experiential Knowledge*	Genuine two-way dialogue allows all RISE participants to cross normal boundaries, respecting different disciplinary knowledge, life experiences, perspectives, and funds of knowledge *to make the invisible visible*. For teachers, this means documenting and building on existing practices (making them more visible to the teachers themselves), and allowing for variation in curriculum implementation and professional development experiences, such that differentiated adult support can be provided. For families, this means making visible the cultural resources in children's homes and communities and empowering parents as advocates for their children and as equal partners with teachers in curriculum development.
2. *Build Shared Understandings Through Active and Collaborative Learning Experiences*	When adults work together on something meaningful that meets a shared goal, within a context where everyone's expertise is valid and needed, they can come to see one another's perspectives and can bridge divides that exist across culturally-established norms and roles. In RISE, joint activities lead to shared understandings about STE, about children's lived experiences, and to attitude shifts that enable the joint construction of culturally-relevant STE curriculum.
3. *Co-construct Meaningful Inquiry for Children Around STE Content*	Nontrivial STE content engages both children and teachers in inquiry-based explorations and discoveries focused on big ideas worthy of teachers' and children's time and effort. Meaningful STE learning experiences are those that are challenging but within reach of young children, that are based in phenomena that children can directly experience, and that are culturally and locally relevant. STE learning also must be connected over time, so that children deepen their understandings of underlying concepts. For example, on neighborhood walks, teachers can take monthly photos of trees, shrubs, and other objects in the environment—both living and nonliving—to make visible to children the ways that their surroundings change or remain stable over time.
4. *Promote a "Living" Curriculum*	Curriculum changes every time a teacher implements it, and grows with children's and teachers' understandings. Any curriculum also occurs in a local context, and therefore, it will evolve and change as it is used in different settings, and over time. What RISE offers is a process approach, guided by national and local STE learning standards (Massachusetts Department of Elementary and Secondary Education, 2016; National Research Council, 2012; National Science Teachers Association, 2014), that is ever-evolving, sustainable, and transportable. Thus, fidelity to the RISE approach is adherence to iterative collaboration in curriculum development and implementation, and to these guiding principles and shared procedures, rather than to specific, prescribed curricular activities or scripts.

The middle portion of the graphic reflects our commitment to relationship- and capacity-building through professional development. First, teachers are connected to the research team and to STE content and pedagogy in *professional development workshops,* which provide for hands-on activities designed to foster teachers' curiosity and comfort with STE. Second, teachers are connected to their STE coach through: *1:1 Coaching sessions,* which provide individualized support for reflective practice; and *professional learning community meetings,* which connect teachers to one another while providing support for building their STE confidence and leadership skills. Third, teachers are connected to families through *joint activities* and *parent-teacher discussion* groups. Over time, the "joint-ness" occurring within these discussions and activities evolves into a level of unprecedented collaboration.

The final part of the graphic shows the ultimate product—a STE curriculum—developed through reciprocal engagement between parents and teachers—that empowers teachers and families to work as equal partners, and that incorporates home and community funds of knowledge into the formal curriculum of the preschool classroom.

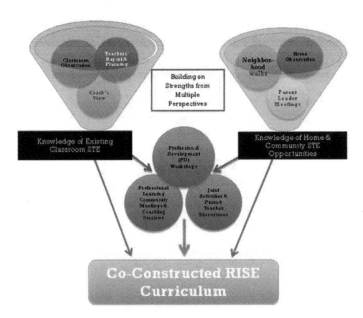

Figure 6.1.   The process of RISE curriculum development through reciprocal engagement between families and teachers to incorporate home and community funds of knowledge.

HOME-SCHOOL COLLABORATION IN THE RISE PROJECT

In the remainder of this chapter, we focus on the home-school collaboration component of the RISE approach. This component is guided by two inter-related experiences—joint activities and parent-teacher discussion groups. Joint activities provide opportunities for families and educators to work together toward a shared goal. It is within joint activities that families and educators come to understand each other, communicate in new ways, and see each other as equal partners (e.g., Rogoff, 2003). Parent-teacher discussion groups provide another opportunity for respectful and reciprocal dialogue. Through conversations about topics that matter to them, teachers and parents come to question their assumptions about one another, and even disagree, while building toward understanding (Adair & Tobin, 2008). Through these two forms of interaction, teachers gain access to what Moll and colleagues (2005) termed "families' funds of knowledge"—immigrant parents' knowledge of the local environment and community, and the expertise families have developed in their everyday home, work, social, and political lives. By understanding and appreciating families' funds of knowledge and the supports already available to students at home and in the community, teachers can make connections between these experiences and the classroom curriculum in ways that are truly significant for students (Civil, 2016).

Essential to the RISE approach, then, is that the home-to-school flow of information is just as important as the school-to-home flow, with a particular focus in RISE on STE learning as the family-school bridge. Home-school collaboration efforts in RISE go well beyond the home extension activities that typically constitute the home involvement component of early childhood curricula. The importance of the *bidirectional* flow of information between home and school is clearly articulated by a RISE teacher as follows:

> *Head Start has an open-door policy.… They always involve parents in the class-room, and ask them to help, and try to give ideas how to help parents with their children at home. But in this project … they're making it a circle. They don't just want teachers to give ideas to the parents and bring [them] home.… They also want us to get ideas from the parents… I think that piece is very important.*

EXAMPLES OF HOME-TO-SCHOOL
CONTRIBUTIONS TO STE CURRICULUM

At the outset of the RISE project, we worked separately with parents and with teachers to establish the foundation for them to work together as equal partners. We held discussions with parent leaders (i.e., individuals who volunteered to serve as our guides) to create a comfortable space for them to share information and strengthen their leadership and advocacy skills. We also created structured opportunities for them to share their funds of knowledge. For example, parent leaders planned the routes for our information-gathering neighborhood walks. Photographs taken during the walks made visible how children's everyday observations of the structures in their built environments were reflected in the forms of their blocks and ramps constructions.

Figure 6.2.   Reflections of tall buildings and bridges observed during neighborhood walks in children's block and ramp play.

We worked with teachers simultaneously, but separately, to help them recognize the power imbalances inherent in the teacher-family relationship and to prepare a space where trust-building and reciprocal dialogue with parents could occur. For example, in preparation for the first joint activity, the research team facilitated teachers' awareness of the need to let parents lead interactions and initiate dialogue. Teachers were asked to "take the back seat," and parents were assigned the role of group facilitators, with support from the researchers. Parent-teacher interactions were thus intentionally "stacked in favor" of parents initially to disrupt the typical dynamic that teachers have more power in home-school relations.

In one such joint activity, parents and teachers created a scrapbook, titled "Our Children's Worlds," depicting what children experience at home and in the classroom, using photos taken during classroom activities, home observations and neighborhood walks. In these scrapbooks, there was a specific focus on objects relevant to STE learning (e.g., a community garden full of opportunities for learning about life science; a playground for discussing ramp structures and elements of engineering design). Captions were developed in parents' home languages, and the completed scrapbooks were made available to children and families within the classrooms. These joint activities illustrate the significance of creating opportunities for parents to share knowledge of their communities and children with teachers in an informal setting.

Figure 6.3.   These are sample pages from the co-constructed books, showing how images from the neighborhood related to children's classroom STE learning. The page on the right contains a caption written in Spanish by a parent that reads, "They are going to start building with pieces of wood…. Here the children are having fun playing."

In another joint activity, parents and teachers worked together to create structures out of recyclable materials that reflected something meaningful about children's cultural and physical communities (see Figure 6.4). While building a model downtown apartment, parents initiated a discussion about the structure and function of roof angles in their homeland, compared to roof angles in their current neighborhood. This information was later incorporated into the curriculum units on structure and function that teachers were implementing with the children.

Figure 6.4.   These photos of parents and teachers were taken during a joint activity aimed at co-constructing meaningful structures from children's environments. On the left, parents and teachers construct a replica of the Great Wall of China, while on the right parents and teachers proudly show their replica of the airport and a soccer field.

Once more balanced relationships between teachers and parents were established, parents and teachers took over the task of co-planning and co-facilitating the parent-teacher discussions and joint activities on their own. Through these dialogues, teachers came to understand more about children's cultures and home lives. This gave teachers an increased ability to draw on children's existing knowledge and skills and families' funds of knowledge when designing curriculum.

For example, in one classroom, during Lunar New Year celebrations, the teacher encouraged children to represent their observations of "lucky bamboo" using recycled objects, tape, and paint. Children applied their knowledge about stable structures to find creative ways to make their bamboo designs stand upright.

Figure 6.5.   This is an example of how an artifact from everyday life (bamboo) was brought into the classroom curriculum on engineering design, to reinforce the concept of stability. This part of the curriculum happened around Lunar New Year celebrations in the children's communities, when lucky bamboo is given as a gift.

Parents, in turn, became comfortable and empowered to engage with teachers and share information about their experiences and their communities. In one parent-teacher discussion group, recognizing connections across each other's unique cultural contexts, parents and teachers shared recipes for soups they make in their homes, which connected to concurrent classroom STE activities concerning states of matter. In other discussions, immigrant parents talked with Head Start teachers (some of whom were immigrants themselves) about barriers they experience to participating in their children's education. By the end of the project, teachers came to appreciate the value of engaging with families in reciprocal dialogue and joint activities, as the quotations below illustrate:

> *Usually in Head Start … we always have the newsletter or activities, handing back to home for the parents, "that's the curriculum we have in school, that's what you can do at home with your kids." But, I am really learning something now. As the teacher we can get activities and ideas from home to school, extend it, and put into the curriculum. We do a lot of involvement, but now it's not just involvement, it's engagement. It's two-way, not one-way.*

> *Meeting with parents at night, was historic; really, really you saw their culture, how much they really do value you. You saw how much they really admired you, and they thought less of themselves, and you are like, "No…" You have to also validate those parents just as much as you validate their children because, they are so special, and they work so hard, so, it's … I … can't even say it, it's like a collaboration that you dreamed about…. Parents need to be understood, too, because they want to help…. The one common goal we have is to see these children succeed.*

The RISE approach is built on the idea that schools can leverage families' unique contributions to children's learning, rather than trying to overwrite them to get children "ready for school.

PUTTING RISE INTO ACTION IN YOUR CLASSROOM

We offer here a few ideas to inspire your own reflective STE practice, broaden your perspective about DLLs, awaken your excitement about the role that families can play in early childhood curriculum, and whet your appetite for more knowledge and skills to enhance the cultural relevance of curriculum for *all* children. Here are a handful of take-aways and actionable steps to consider:

1. **Connect new concepts to prior experiences and familiar knowledge.** Children learn more effectively when prior experiences are

reflected in the formal classroom curriculum. For White, middle-income children, much about school is familiar. But for non-White, immigrant, and/or low-income children, this might not be the case. The U.S. classroom contains many unfamiliar objects (e.g., "water table"), routines (e.g., "circle time"), and social expectations (e.g., raising your hand to request a speaking turn). To facilitate children's learning, educators must resist stereotypical views of families and work to bridge the experiences across children's home and school contexts. They can do this by seeking information about home, community, and cultural assets upon which authentic curricular connections can be built. We call this the *home-to-school* approach. By framing family engagement as emphasizing information flowing from the home to the school, in addition to the more typical school-to-home flow, teachers can make a subtle yet profound shift in their expectations about how to engage families. As teachers spend more time getting to know families' experiential knowledge, what children see and do every day, and what family routines are important, possibilities emerge for incorporating these into the curriculum. Children's homes and neighborhoods become rich resources for STE curriculum.

To get started, teachers can use home visits at the beginning of the school year to look for important "tools" in the home that can be brought into the classroom related to a particular STE concept (e.g., special spoons for noodle soups or chopsticks provide examples of the relationship between structure and function). Another common routine among early childhood classrooms is doing neighborhood walks; teachers can readily identify relevant STE concepts in children's communities (e.g., the ramps in the block center relate to ramps coming off service trucks, at curb cutouts, and going into the grocery store). Even if such walks are not a part of school routine, teachers can do their own neighborhood walks to look for natural STE learning connections based on what children see in their everyday lives.

2. **Create family engagement opportunities that are perceived as "meaningful" by parents and teachers.** All too often, the expectations for engaging families feel forced to teachers and, literally, foreign to families. There has been much acknowledgment recently that *relationally-situated* and *culturally-situated* engagement efforts are needed. Relationally-situated engagement efforts involve activities planned between educators and families through joint engagement that result in "trust building" (Kim & Sheridan, 2015). Culturally-situated engagement efforts ensure their relevance to children's home and community lives (McWayne, Doucet, & Mistry, in prepa-

ration) RISE encourages both relationally-situated and culturally-situated engagement through joint activities and parent-teacher discussion groups. We have seen how joint activities can foster non-hierarchical, reciprocal dialogue between parents and teachers, thus building strong relationships as equal partners. These joint activities and parent-teacher discussion groups also offer teachers access to the funds of knowledge of families that they can then connect to the curriculum. In this way, relational engagement in RISE has a specific purpose—to build bridges across (sometimes disparate) cultural funds of knowledge in order to facilitate connections on behalf of children's learning. We believe that changes in teachers' attitudes and practice occur in active relationship-building with parents that has these elements. We encourage you to host your own joint activities as a way to build more trusting relationships with *families as equal partners* in the process of educating their children.

3. **Ensure the regular support and commitment of program leadership for effective home-school collaboration.** Teachers often feel that unrealistic expectations have been placed on them with no real guidance or structural support to foster or sustain their efforts. Just as teachers need ongoing, regular supports to integrate STE teaching and learning into their classrooms, they also need ongoing supports to effectively and meaningfully engage with immigrant families. In RISE, this support is provided specifically to ensure that STE curriculum is responsive to children in the context of their families and communities. For example, our partner directors designated personnel time and physical space for joint activities and parent-teacher discussion groups. However, many opportunities already exist within program structures to encourage this responsive support. For example, Head Start programs have *policy councils* at the grantee level and *parent committees* in every program. These shared governance bodies can not only serve to endorse innovative family engagement practices, but can also become actively engaged in efforts to ensure cultural relevance of curriculum. Teachers can discuss their ideas for this and co-construct new ideas with this body. In addition, program directors can develop a staff position specifically for supporting family engagement, or can protect the time within an already existing formal role for supporting teachers in this work.

CONCLUSIONS

A one-size-fits-all model of family engagement will not meet the needs of the socioculturally diverse families served by our nation's early childhood programs today. RISE recognizes that—by building on children's existing knowledge, including resources within their families and cultural communities, and connecting STE curriculum content to that familiar knowledge—we can open the innovation pipeline for *all* children. We accomplish this in RISE through fostering family-school connections built on trust and mutual respect, so that teachers can recognize and incorporate the rich cognitive and cultural resources of families, while also coming to view families as equal partners in supporting DLL children's learning. Our hope is that other early childhood professionals will find what is relayed here to be inspiring and useful as they go about the intellectually rigorous and impactful work of educating our nation's most important citizens—its young children!

NOTES

1. The intervention discussed in this chapter, RISE, does not directly address mathematics, so our focus is on the "STE" part of STEM education.
2. The RISE Project was funded by the National Science Foundation (Grant # 1221065; 1621161), the Brady Education Foundation, the Heising-Simons Foundation, as well as by private support from Ellen R. Cohen to Tufts University.

REFERENCES

Adair, J., & Tobin, J. (2008). Listening to the voices of immigrant parents. In C. Genishi & A. Lin Goodwin (Eds.), *Diversities in early childhood education: Rethinking and doing* (pp. 137–150). New York, NY: Routledge.

American Psychological Association, Presidential Task Force on Educational Disparities. (2012). *Ethnic and racial disparities in education: Psychology's contributions to understanding and reducing disparities.* Retrieved from http://www.apa.org/ed/resources/racial-disparities.aspx

Bustamante, A., White, L., & Greenfield, D. B. (2016). Approaches to learning and school readiness in Head Start: Applications to preschool science. *Learning and Individual Differences, 56,* 112–118. doi:10.1016/j.lindif.2016.10.012

Civic Impulse. (2017). *S. 1177–114th Congress: Every Student Succeeds Act.* Retrieved from https://www.govtrack.us/congress/bills/114/s1177

Civil, M. (2016). STEM learning research through a funds of knowledge lens. *Cultural Studies of Science Education, 11*(1), 41–59. doi:10.1007/s11422-014-9648-2

Civil, M., & Andrade, R. (2003). Collaborative practice with parents: The role of the researcher as mediator. In A. Peter-Koop, V. Santos-Wagner, C. Breen, & A. Begg (Eds.), *Collaboration in teacher education: Examples from the context of mathematics education* (pp. 153–168). Boston, MA: Kluwer.

Delgado-Gaitan, C. (1991). Involving parents in the schools: A process of empowerment. *American Journal of Education*, *100*(1), 20–46. doi:https://doi.org/10.1086/444003

Doucet, F. (2011). (Re)Constructing home and school: Immigrant parents, agency, and the (un)desirability of bridging multiple worlds. *Teachers College Record*, *113*(12), 2705–2738. Retrieved from http://www.tcrecord.org (ID Number: 16203)

Espinosa, L., Laffey, J., & Whittaker, T. (2006). *Language minority children analysis: Focus on technology use*. Washington, DC: National Center for Education Statistics.

French, L. (2004). Science as the center of a coherent, integrated, early childhood curriculum. *Early Childhood Research Quarterly*, *19*(1), 138–149. doi:https://doi.org/10.1016/j.ecresq.2004.01.004

Gelman, R., & Brenneman, K. (2011). Science classrooms as learning labs. In N. Stein & S. Raudenbusch (Eds.), *Developmental science goes to school* (pp. 113–126). New York, NY: Routledge.

Gelman, R., Brenneman, K., Macdonald, G., & Roman, M. (2009). *Preschool pathways to science (PrePS): Facilitating scientific ways of thinking, talking, doing, and understanding*. Baltimore, MD: Brookes.

Ginsburg-Block, M., Manz, P. H., & McWayne, C. (2010). Partnering with families to foster early achievement in reading and mathematics. In A. L. Reschly & S. Christenson (Eds.), *The handbook on school family partnerships for promoting student competence* (pp. 176–203). Oxford, England: Routledge/Taylor and Francis Group.

Greenfield, D., Jirout, J., Dominguez, X., Greenberg, A., Maier, M., & Fuccillo, J. (2009). Science in the preschool classroom: A programmatic research agenda to improve science readiness. *Early Education and Development*, *20*, 238–264. doi:10.1080/10409280802595441

Hill, N. E. (2010). Culturally-based worldviews, family processes, and family-school interactions. In S. L. Christenson & A. L. Reschly (Eds.), *Handbook of school-family partnership* (pp. 101–127). New York, NY: Routledge.

Kim, E. M., & Sheridan, S. M. (2015). Foundational aspects of family-school connections: Definitions, conceptual frameworks, and research needs. In S. M. Sheridan & E. M. Kim (Eds.), *Research on family-school partnerships: An interdisciplinary examination of state of the science and critical needs: Foundational Aspects of Family-School Partnerships* (Vol. 1, pp. 1–14) New York, NY: Springer.

Mapp, K. L., & Hong, S. (2010). Debunking the myth of the hard-to-reach parent. In A. L. Reschly & S. Christenson (Eds.). *The handbook on school family partnerships for promoting student competence* (pp. 176–203). Oxford, England: Routledge/Taylor and Francis Group.

Massachusetts Department of Elementary and Secondary Education. (2016). *2016 Massachusetts science and technology/engineering curriculum framework*. Malden, MA: Massachusetts Department of Elementary and Secondary Education. Retrieved from http://www.doe.mass.edu/frameworks/scitech/2016-04.pdf

Matthews, H., & Ewen, D. (2006). *Reaching all children? Understanding early care and education participation among immigrant families*. Washington, DC: Center for Law and Social Policy. Retrieved from https://eric.ed.gov/?id=ED489574

Mattingly, D. J., Prislin, R., McKenzie, T. L., Rodriguez, J. L., & Kayzar, B. (2002). Evaluating evaluations: The case of parent involvement programs. *Review of Educational Research*, *72*, 549–576.

McWayne, C. M. (2015). Family-school partnerships in a context of urgent engagement: Rethinking models, measurement, and meaningfulness. In S. Sheridan (Ed.), *Research on family-school partnerships: An interdisciplinary examination of state of the science and critical needs* (pp. 105–124). Switzerland: Springer International.

McWayne, C. M., Doucet, F., & Mistry, J. (in preparation). Family-school partnerships in ethnocultural communities: Redirecting conceptual frameworks, research methods, and intervention efforts by rotating our lens. To appear in C. McWayne, F. Doucet, & S. Sheridan (Eds.), *Research on family-school partnerships: Understanding ethnocultural diversity and the home-to-school link*. New York, NY: Springer.

Moll, L. C., Amanti, C., Neff, D., & González, N. (2005). Funds of knowledge for teaching: Using a qualitative approach to connect homes and classrooms. In N. González, L. C. Moll, & C. Amanti (Eds.), *Funds of knowledge: Theorizing practices in households, communities, and classrooms* (pp. 71–87). Mahwah, NJ: Lawrence Erlbaum Associates.

National Research Council. (2012). *A framework for K–12 science education: Practices, crosscutting concepts, and core ideas*. Committee on a Conceptual Framework for New K–12 Science Education Standards. Board on Science Education, Division of Behavioral and Social Sciences and Education. Washington, DC: The National Academies Press.

National Science Board. (2009). *National Science Board STEM education recommendations for the President-Elect Obama administration*. Retrieved from www.nsf.gov/nsb/publications/2009/01_10_stem_rec_obama.pdf

National Science Teachers Association (NSTA). (2014). NSTA position statement: Early childhood science education. Retrieved from http://www.nsta.org/about/positions/earlychildhood.aspx

Nayfeld, I., Fuccillo, J., & Greenfield, D. B. (2013). Executive functions in early learning: Extending the relationship between executive functions and school readiness to science. *Learning and Individual Differences*, *26*, 81–88. doi:https://doi.org/10.1016/j.lindif.2013.04.011

Park, M., & McHuge, M. (2014). *Immigrant parents and early childhood programs: Addressing barriers of literacy, culture, and systems knowledge*. Washington, DC: Migration Policy Institute. Retrieved from http://www.migrationpolicy.org/research/immigrant-parents-early-childhood-programs-barriers

Pattnaik, J. (2003). Learning about the "other": Building a case for intercultural understanding among minority children. *Childhood Education*, *79*(4), 204–211. doi:http://dx.doi.org/10.1080/00094056.2003.10521194

Ramirez, A. Y. F. (2003). Dismay and disappointment: Parental involvement of Latino immigrant parents. *The Urban Review*, *35*(2), 93–110. doi:https://doi.org/10.1023/A:1023705511946

Reardon, S., & Galindo, C. (2009). The Hispanic-White achievement gap in math and reading in the elementary grades. *American Educational Research Journal*, *46*(3), 853–891. doi:https://doi.org/10.3102/0002831209333184

Rogoff, B. (2003). *The cultural nature of human development.* Oxford, England: Oxford University Press.

Thomas, W. P., & Collier, V. P. (2002). *A national study of school effectiveness for language minority students' long-term academic achievement.* Washington, DC: Office of Educational Research and Improvement. Retrieved from http://eric.ed.gov/?id=ED475048

CHAPTER 7

COLLECTIVE IMPACT APPROACH TO STEM

The Case of Iridescent

Tara Chklovski and Maggie Jaris

What I like the most is I get to sit with my kids and work with them which we hardly do at home. So I say that's why it's called Family Science because it's the family that gets together and builds stuff, stuff that you usually don't get to do at home that often. So it is a time where you spend time with your kids and doing what they like.

—Parent from Iridescent Family Science Program

Low-income students of color and immigrants face major barriers to a quality education (American Psychological Association, 2010). Insufficient public education funding, lack of educational supports (Duncan & Murnane, 2014; U.S. Department of Education, 2011a, 2011b), language differences (Motamedi, Singh, & Thompson, 2016; O'Conner, Abedi, & Tung, 2012), and transportation challenges (Robinson, 2015) too often prevent these young people from attaining the education they need to enter a 21st century workforce. Despite years of education reform, opportunity gaps between advantaged and disadvantaged communities continue to grow.

In no area of education are these disparities more evident than in science, technology, engineering, and math (STEM). By fourth grade, many low-

Promising Practices for Engaging Families in STEM Learning, pp. 99–113
Copyright © 2018 by Information Age Publishing

99

income students are already behind in reading and math (Child Trends, 2013) and are less likely to be exposed to STEM in any meaningful way. They lack access to mentors, tutors and other educational supports and, as a result, likely will not see STEM as a career path. All of this contributes to the growing racial/ethnic and gender gap in STEM and technology fields, where there is significant job growth but a shortage of skilled workers. In a globalized world where innovation and technology are drivers of growth and opportunity, we are leaving behind an entire generation of potential leaders.

Many interventions aimed at addressing the shortage in STEM start with the formal learning environment. However, most people (even those who attend graduate school) spend only 18–20% of their entire lives in formal learning environments (LIFE Center, 2005). The majority of our time is instead spent in informal, choice-based, self-directed learning environments. Because of this, family engagement—which is associated with higher academic achievement and social competence, lower rates of adolescent high-risk behavior, greater success in postsecondary education, and stronger careers—emerges as a high leverage point to increase STEM outcomes among all students, but especially those who are most at risk (Christenson & Sheridan, 2001; Henderson & Mapp, 2002; Jeynes, 2005).

However, asking parents to play a key role in STEM programs can be challenging (Goodall & Montgomery, 2013; Hornby & Lafaele, 2011; Lopez, Gonzalez-Barrera, & Patten, 2013; Rogoff, Turkanis, & Bartlett, 2002; Smith, 2014; Zickuhr & Smith, 2012). Parents might feel discomfort or have low confidence in their own STEM proficiency. For parents to meaningfully support their children's STEM education, they need to become STEM leaders and innovators themselves (Dierking & Falk, 1994; National Research Council, 2009). Moreover, developing self-motivated learners takes time, practice, and repeated modeling of the core character traits of curiosity, creativity, and perseverance. Thus, efforts to engage families in STEM learning needs to take place over many years.

Finally, for family engagement in STEM to make a difference, all parts of the educational continuum must improve at the same time. No single organization can improve student achievement alone. This concept is called "Collective Impact," and refers to the specific approach of solving social problems—such as reducing gaps in STEM achievement between low and upper income students—by bringing together a group of stakeholders to commit to a common agenda (Kania & Kramer, 2011).

In this chapter we explore how Iridescent, a global STEM-education nonprofit focused on using engineering and technology for social change and transforming the opportunities available to disadvantaged young people, is an example of a strong family engagement and a model of collective impact. We first lay out the Iridescent approach, and then provide two case studies of the impact of our work.

Iridescent and Curiosity Machine

Iridescent was started in 2006 with the goal to develop a large scale, cost-effective two-generation model of STEM education. Our model relies on three very different groups of people: engineers, educators, and parents from underserved communities. Collectively, these partners are the very essence of a cognitively diverse group, bringing together different languages, nationalities, perspectives, education and socioeconomic levels, heuristics, technological literacies, and learning speeds. Even though these groups seem very different, in actuality they have two very important characteristics in common: (1) an interest in helping children become self-driven learners, and (2) a certain comfort with risk and trying new things. Our program leverages these commonalities.

The Model Elements

Iridescent's Curiosity Machine Family Program serves families with children in grades kindergarten through fifth grade. The Curiosity Machine Family Program has four main elements: family design nights, virtual design, parent leadership, and scientist, engineering and educator training.

Family Design Nights. Iridescent brings underserved families together as a group, in person, over 5 weeks to do open-ended engineering design challenges with the help of scientists and engineers who mentor the families as they build. Sessions are held in familiar locations such as schools, often during dinner time; meals are provided for families. This practical aspect of holding sessions during dinner time and providing dinner is the key reason of this program's success because it frees up time from meal preparation and directs it to meaningful, family learning.

In a typical course, engineers spend the first 5 minutes of the session briefly introducing their work, and then show a video related to their area of expertise. Following the video, engineers introduce a design challenge. Design challenges are open-ended hands-on projects that help students understand specific science and engineering concepts using inexpensive materials. For instance, the Planting Machine challenge asks students to build a moving cardboard vehicle that drops "seeds" at defined intervals with accuracy. Families spend an hour planning, designing, building, and testing their design while the engineers walk around the room helping them. After testing and redesign, engineers lead an "Analyze and Reflect" exercise with the participants and encourage them to keep improving their models at home.

Virtual Design. In the second element of the model, following the community in-person learning experience, families disperse and continue to learn by doing more design challenges at home via the Curiosity Machine virtual platform. This blended learning model ensures that families have opportunities both in the real world and virtually to explore and practice STEM. The online platform (www.curiositymachine.org) gives students and families access to curriculum, instructional videos, trained engineers and scientists who serve as virtual STEM mentors, and additional resources. Students can upload videos of their own projects in response to a design challenge and virtual mentors can provide personalized feedback to them on how best to improve their design.

Parent Leadership. In the third program element, parents are trained to become leaders in their school community and to organize logistics for an ongoing program. Parents receive a combination of online (https://www.curiositymachine.org/parent-training-intro-series/) and in-person training to establish a vibrant STEM learning community at their school. The first stage of the training is conducted in-person with parents who express interest in becoming Curiosity Machine parent leaders. The 5 hour training covers basic physics concepts as well as pedagogical concepts such as how we learn (National Research Council, 2000), the importance of adopting a "growth mindset" (Dweck, 2007), learning to identify and address negative attributes, especially around interest and ability in STEM (Schunk & Pintrich, 2008), asking open-ended questions (McComas & Abraham, 2004), and encouraging and supporting youth to develop their sense of self-efficacy (Bandura, 1997). The goal of this training is to help Parent Leaders increase their own sense of self-efficacy and become empowered to train and support other parents in their school community. In effect, parents take on the role of program leaders for an afterschool program—they take responsibility for recruiting families for the ongoing Curiosity Machine program, coordinating dinners, managing translations from one language to another, buying materials for the design challenges, and registering families at each session and onto the online platform. Parents can also go on to co-facilitate the sessions, leading or co-leading the presentations of the design challenges along with another parent leader or an educator.

Engineer and Educator Training. Iridescent builds the capacity of engineers, scientists, and educators to support family engagement in STEM learning. Engineers and scientists who participate in the program as instructors and mentors go through a technical communication training consisting of seven modules that cover topics including introducing yourself and your work in a simple language, interacting with families in a culturally sensitive and warm manner, and being aware of stereotypes and gender biases and how to address them. Engineers are volunteers from local corporations and recruitment is either grass-roots and employee driven or led by Iridescent in partnership with the leadership of the corporation. All volunteer engineers are required to complete the 5–10-hour training. Iridescent also offers training for interested educators. Training is conducted either in-person or online and consists of scaffolded engineering design units (https://www.curiositymachine.org/units/) that educators can use to gradually increase the complexity of content for their students. Iridescent strives to make sure the initial trainings with engineers, educators, and parents happen in-person, and to make sure that there is a chance for educators to meet and connect with engineers before the first session of the program. Educators and engineers are co-facilitators of the program, sharing presentation duties and management responsibilities, and it is key that they understand this relationship, connect with each other and agree on each group's responsibilities before the first session. This early connection and shared understanding is also key to the sustainability of the partnership and program over the long-term. Following the initial training, Iridescent offers support through online means, be it a webinar or video training, or ongoing e-mail and phone exchanges.

Curiosity Machine in Action

Below we provide two case studies of how the Iridescent Curiosity Machine Family Program has been implemented in two different communities and explore implementation successes, challenges, and outcomes in both.

Case Study 1: The "Be a Scientist" Project

Be a Scientist! was a 5-year longitudinal study, sponsored by the National Science Foundation, where undergraduate engineering students in Los Angeles and New York City offered Curiosity Machine programming to underserved families with children in grades one through five in partnership with local museums and schools (including University of Southern California's School of Cinematic Arts and the Viterbi School of Engineering, The Cooper Union, Los Angeles Natural History Museum, and New York Hall of Science). In total, Iridescent served 2,173 participants, including children and families, for 18,628 hours over the 5 years. A few families participated for all 5 years—a notable achievement (Pierson, Momoh, & Hupert, 2015). The evaluation of the project showed the program has a positive influence on children, families, and engineers. The vast majority of school-age students who participated indicated that as a result of their participation they understood science and engineering better (90%) and that they had a better understanding of what jobs are available in those fields (88%). Students also responded that they were more excited about doing challenging activities (94%) and that they were more interested in their science class at school (86%). One fifth grade girl talked about how Curiosity Machine helped her think like a scientist at school:

> *When we build something and it's not made correctly, we have to keep on trying to get it because you have to have patience to do it. And my teacher says that scientists don't build things at one try. They take many tries to build it.*

Overwhelmingly, parents and guardians reported positive changes in their own behavior since participating in the Curiosity Machine program. Over 90% of all families agreed or strongly agreed that since participating in the program they would engage in more science related activities like visiting zoos, reading books about science, watching science related TV shows and doing hands on science activities at home. Similarly, 94% indicated that they would ask their child more questions about science class, and 91% said they would encourage their child to pursue an education or career in science or engineering. Families also saw the value of the program in changing the school climate and helping their children succeed. One mother said:

> *They have done better projects at school because she participated in the Family Science Program. The program gives her ideas that she didn't have before. For example electricity, she understood it better in school because she was participating in Curiosity Machine.*

Parents who were part of the project for five consecutive years shared what they enjoyed most about coming to the program. Overall the parents liked being able to do something together as a family. Parents also liked watching their children working through challenging projects. A mother of fifth grade twin girls shared that what she enjoyed most about attending Curiosity Machine was,

> *Seeing their faces when they learn something new or whenever they see something that interests them … seeing them try and whenever they get something wrong, they don't cry or they don't put that face, that sad face. They're like, "Oh let's try it again, let's do it again. We have to do this."*

An overwhelming majority of the mentoring undergraduate engineering students reported having a positive experience teaching and mentoring the families. Eighty percent of the engineers described the experience as "a great opportunity to learn outside the usual classroom," "a good break from typical engineering classes," and "fun and challenging in a way engineers typically aren't exposed to." The undergraduates appreciated that the experience allowed them to gain teaching skills and confidence in relaying what they do. Specifically, student engineers found that the experience improved their communication skills, gave them a better understanding of teaching practices, and increased their knowledge of the local community.

Case Study 2: Boeing, Iridescent, and the Washington Alliance for Better Schools

In the winter of 2014, Iridescent partnered with Boeing and the nonprofit Washington Alliance for Better Schools (WABS) in the Puget Sound area of Washington State. Boeing—one of the world's largest aerospace companies and manufacturer of airplanes—was seeking skills-based volunteering opportunities for its employees as well as opportunities to deepen its long-standing relationship with the community. WABS, a collaborative of eleven school districts that works to empower and build leadership among parents who are immigrants and English as second language learners, was looking for new ways to engage families in children's learning in meaningful ways. A partnership among the three entities was a perfect match and gave Iridescent the opportunity to gradually test shifting responsibilities for leading the courses from the engineers to parents themselves.

Stage 1: Winter 2014 and Spring 2015. The implementation began with one school in the WABS network and focused on training Boeing engineers to lead Curiosity Machine family courses and educating parents to support these sessions. Iridescent trained the Boeing engineers to develop design challenges based on their own work, and to share their experience with the families. For example, two Boeing engineers created a "Hack a Box" challenge in which engineers challenged children and families to think about how to prevent hackers from accessing planes' computers and to develop alarm system networks to notify Boeing of any intrusions. Iridescent also trained parents to support the engineers by managing the logistics of the course. This stage allowed each implementation partner to become comfortable working together.

Stage 2: Fall 2015. In the fall of 2015, Stage 2 of the implementation began. This stage focused on training the parent leaders to present the design challenges to the families. Iridescent trained parents at two different schools in the WABS network. Parents now played the primary role in recruiting other parents, supporting the logistics of collecting materials, and teaching and leading Curiosity Machine family courses, while engineers took on a supporting role, working with families during the building stage of each session.[1] Iridescent led a full-day training with parents covering how to teach and present design challenges. Engineers from Boeing were also trained to provide support during course sessions. This training was virtual, lasted several hours, and many of the same volunteers from Stage 1 continued to volunteer in Stage 2.

Stage 3: Spring 2016. Stage 3 focused on scaling the implementation and fully transferring leadership responsibilities to the parents and support responsibilities to the WABS staff. Iridescent trained a large cohort of teachers from 10 different schools. The training was improved, taking into consideration the feedback received during Stage 2. Notably this included adding additional webinars throughout the year to support parents. During these webinars, parents would build a design challenge and receive immediate feedback and support from Iridescent staff via videoconferencing tools. Parents also practiced delivering their content-focused presentations and received individual feedback from Iridescent staff. Iridescent introduced these webinars after realizing that a single in-person training did not provide enough support to parents with non-technical backgrounds. Iridescent recognized that parents wanted to practice their presentations and receive feedback from Iridescent staff and realized that these support sessions should happen 1–2 weeks before the actual program sessions to best bolster parents' confidence and skills. It was not feasible to fly staff to the schools before each session, so Iridescent introduced webinars that made use of video-conferencing tools and allowed for two-way communication. These webinars proved to be an adequate way to support the parents and were effective in developing their own sense of self-efficacy as STEM facilitators and leaders. Iridescent also made recommendations for organizing parent leaders, suggesting schools select one parent leader to facilitate the STEM content and assign two parent leaders to facilitate the building sessions and manage logistics.

Taken as a whole the initiative was successful. Over the course of the implementation, more than 500 children and 300 parents participated in Curiosity Machine family course programs at WABS schools. The program as experienced by the families remain unchanged through the various shifts of responsibility and capacity building stages. Many parents developed into leaders at their children's' schools (a few parent leaders were even later hired as parent coordinators by the schools!) and developed professional skills and experience. WABS works with many immigrant families, and in this implementation, many of the parents were mothers who did not work outside the home—this program helped them develop confidence and skills and provided opportunities to apply those skills in more formalized roles within their children's schools.

Moving forward, sustainability and support will come from WABS staff members and parent leaders who are familiar with the model. The program has been positively received by the school district, which had supported the program because it involved parent leaders and development for those parent leaders so the program could continue. Iridescent's last trainings were held in early 2016, and as of September 2017, the program is still running. Sustainability was built into the program and the community from the outset because it was made clear that Iridescent would primarily play a support and capacity building role. Another reason why the program has been sustainable is because WABS has been working with its communities for many years and has long-standing relationships built on trust with them.

There is additional evidence that the initiative influenced the participating engineers, too. Boeing conducted a preliminary internal study evaluating the impact of Iridescent's model on 26 of their engineers. 82% of participating engineers said that developing and teaching the engineering design challenges increased their own creativity and communication skills (Richey, Gupta, Meyers, Zender, & Vermeer, 2015).

LESSONS LEARNED

In 10 years of developing and adapting a collective impact model that can work with large school networks and in small communities, we at Iridescent have learned some surprising things in STEM education and family engagement:

- **Training matters:** Collective impact models bring together very different groups of people, and we quickly realized we needed to do significant training for each group on how to communicate effectively. Our trainings had to cover communicating with both children and adults from different backgrounds. This meant that trainings had to cover ideas like open-ended questions and fostering growth mindsets, as well as ideas like empathy, tolerance, and bias. Engineers and scientists (especially from corporations) typically do not interact with underserved communities or share technical elements of their work with grandparents or parents. Similarly, grandparents and parents from underserved communities do not usually interact with engineers and scientists in a social setting. We learned that we needed to prepare all stakeholders to talk to and connect with one another and built this into our trainings. We allowed extra time for the groups to meet each other before they started the training and had them go through ice-breakers together.
- **Pay attention to logistics:** Underserved parents are very motivated and willing to access opportunities for high quality education for their children. However, it is critical to address basic logistical bar-

riers by providing dinner at the evening Curiosity Machine Family Programs, holding the sessions at familiar places, translating the content of the presentation and instructions for the activities, providing tutorials to use technology, and ensuring the materials used in the design challenges are low cost. We learned that it is important for each group to have a point person representing them and meeting regularly with the other points of contact, planning out the details of the program.

- **This work takes time:** We also learned that it takes a long time to successfully implement a collective impact model. For instance, our implementation with WABS and Boeing took 3 years. During the first year, everyone got to know each other, and experience the value of this program. The second year was focused on helping parents become more confident and skilled at delivering the content and helping each group develop their self-efficacy and leadership skills by running more of the program themselves. Finally, the third year focused primarily on getting each group comfortable using online technologies and platforms through which they could access further content, training and analytics. To help ensure similar projects' longevity, support and encourage engineers and parents to develop a bond, frame the program so it is clear that it is the engineers, parents, and educators who are the partners and that Iridescent/the support organization is just facilitating the program as it gets off the ground. Iridescent has also found success in motivating each stakeholder to continue working with the program in the long term by sharing the impact the program is having. We recommend sharing the specific skills students will be developing, the concepts they will be learning, and translating those skills into clear outcomes so that all stakeholders see the vision of the program as a whole.

- **Document and Disseminate Results:** Although we were not always able to execute on this, we saw the long-lasting effects of documentation and dissemination of results. We learned that it is important to have a "Celebration of Learning" event (with music and food!) that brings the whole community together to celebrate the collective effort. The social, emotional, and physiological elements of this community celebration are critical to helping the program grow and thrive into the next year. Alongside this, it is important to have a dedicated person taking good photographs and documenting the stories of impact so that they can be shared with the local press and each group's dissemination channels. This type of impact reporting provides positive feedback to the collective and motivates them to continue investing time and effort in the multi-year project.

- **Actively Seek Funding and Define Roles Over the Course of the Project:** An unexpected consequence of the 3-year timescale of our partnership with Boeing was the awkward conversations related to funding and resources that arose in year two of an implementation. For each of our partnerships, we did not expect how long it would take to change the mindsets of each group, and as a result, we didn't plan for continued support and training in years two and three. Our strong recommendation to others working on similar collective impact models in STEM would be to convene and plan out what the program looks like in years two and three, whose roles will change and in what manner, and where the funding for the program will be coming from. See Table 7.1 for a suggested year-by-year breakdown.

It took us 10 years to develop a strong, customizable collective impact model, and we are still refining it. We are hopeful that in sharing the lessons that we have learned, we can encourage others to adopt similar models and together work to inspire and prepare young people everywhere to self-direct their learning and apply their passion so that they too can tackle the grand challenges of their time.

Table 7.1.
Tips For Building a Collective Impact Model For STEM in Your Community

Year 1	Year 2	Year 3
Identify a corporation or university in your community to bring subject matter expertise in the form of mentors, as well as potential funding.	Provide capacity building, and technology training to each group.	Plan for sustainability of the program and sustaining family engagement.
Identify a community partner—a school or library—that aligns with your overall goals and constraints.	In addition to the program lead from each group, identify an overall leader who can plan for the sustainability of the program.	Plan for the third in-person program implementation period and ongoing online learning.
Identify a champion from each institution to recruit engineers and parents.	Plan for the second in-person program implementation.	Transition to less intensive support, and prepare other leaders.
Document and share program results with all group members.	Document and share program results.	Document and share program results.
Bring each group together and set the collective impact goal and intermediate milestones. Train each group, and implement the first program within 3–5 months of initial outreach to maintain momentum. Debrief, share results with all, and start planning for the second year.	Debrief and plan for the third stage of work.	

NOTE

1. Check out a video of families building and designing using the online platform at: https://www.youtube.com/watch?v=t_x9fL0MF0w

REFERENCES

American Psychological Association. (2010, May 27). *Education and socioeconomic status*. Retrieved from http://www.apa.org/pi/ses/resources/publications/education.aspx

Bandura, A. (1997). *Self-efficacy: The exercise of control*. New York: W.H. Freeman.

Child Trends. (2013, February). *Science proficiency: Indicators on children and youth*. Child Trends Data Bank. Retrieved from https://www.childtrends.org/wp-content/uploads/2012/10/10_Science_Proficiency.pdf

Christenson, S. L., & Sheridan, S. M. (2001). *Schools and families: Creating essential connections for learning*. New York: Guilford Press.

Dierking, L. D., & Falk, J. H. (1994). Family behavior and learning in informal science settings: A review of the research. *Science Education, 78*(1), 57–72. doi:10.1002/sce.3730780104

Duncan, G. J., & Murnane, R. (2014, March 28). *Growing income inequality threatens American education*. Retrieved from http://www.edweek.org/ew/articles/2014/03/01/kappan_duncanmurnane.html

Dweck, C. (2007). *Mindset: The new psychology of success*, New York: Ballantine Books.

Goodall, J., & Montgomery, C. (2013). Parental involvement to parental engagement: A continuum. *Educational Review, 66*(4), 399–410. doi:http://dx.doi.org/10.1080/00131911.2013.781576

Henderson, A. T., & Mapp K. L. (2002). *A new wave of evidence: The impact of school, family, and community connections on student achievement*. Austin, TX: Southwest Educational Development Laboratory.

Hornby, G., & Lafaele, R. (2011). Barriers to parental involvement in education: an explanatory model. *Educational Review, 63*(1), 37–52. doi:10.1080/00131911.2010.488049

Jeynes, W. H. (2005). A meta-analysis of the relation of parental involvement to urban elementary school student academic achievement. *Urban Education, 40*, 237–269. doi:https://doi.org/10.1177/0042085905274540

Kania, J., & Kramer, M. (2011). Collective impact. *Stanford Social Innovation Review, 9*(1), 36–41. Retrieved from http://c.ymcdn.com/sites/www.lano.org/resource/dynamic/blogs/20131007_093137_25993.pdf

LIFE Center. (2005). *The LIFE Center's lifelong and lifewide learning diagram* [Visualization of the amount of time people spend learning in formal and informal learning environments.]. Retrieved from http://life-slc.org/about/about.html

Lopez, M. H., Gonzalez-Barrera, A., & Patten, E. (2013, March 7). *Closing the digital divide: Latinos and technology adoption*. Pew Research Center. Retrieved from http://www.pewhispanic.org/2013/03/07/closing-the-digital-divide-latinos-and-technology-adoption/

McComas, W. F., & Abraham, L. (2004). *Asking more effective questions*. Los Angeles, CA: Rossier School of Education, University of Southern California.

Motamedi, J. G., Singh, M., & Thompson, K. D. (2016, May). *English learner student characteristics and time to reclassification: An example from Washington state (REL 2016-128)*. Washington, DC: U.S. Department of Education, Institute of Education Sciences, National Center for Education Evaluation and Regional Assistance, Regional Educational Laboratory Northwest. Retrieved from https://ies.ed.gov/ncee/edlabs/regions/northwest/pdf/REL_2016128.pdf

National Research Council (2000). *How people learn: Brain, mind, experience, and school*. Washington, DC: The National Academies Press. Retrieved from https://doi.org/10.17226/9853

National Research Council. (2009). *Learning science in informal environments: People, places, and pursuits*. In P. Bell, B. Lewenstein, A. W. Shouse, & M. A. Feder (Eds.), *Committee on learning science in informal environments*. Washington, DC: National Academies Press.

O'Conner, R., Abedi, J., & Tung, S. (2012, April). *A descriptive analysis of enrollment and achievement among English language learner students in Pennsylvania. (Issues and Answers Report, REL 2012–No. 127)*. Washington, DC: U.S. Department of Education, Institute of Education Sciences, National Center for Education Evaluation and Regional Assistance, Regional Educational Laboratory Mid-Atlantic. Retrieved from https://ies.ed.gov/ncee/edlabs/regions/midatlantic/pdf/REL_2012127.pdf

Pierson, E., Momoh, L., & Hupert, N. (2015). *Summative evaluation report for the Be A Scientist! project's Family Science Program*. New York, NY: EDC Center for Children and Technology.

Richey, M., Gupta, D., O'Mahony, T. K., Meyers, L. E., Zender, F., & Vermeer, D. L. (2015, June). *The business case for engineering skills-based volunteerism in K–12 education*. Paper presented at 122nd ASEE Annual Conference & Exposition, Seattle, WA.

Robinson, R. (2015, January 29). *Transportation challenges complicate school choice for SF students*. San Francisco Public Press. Retrieved from http://sfpublicpress.org/news/2015-01/transportation-challenges-complicate-school-choice-for-sf-students

Rogoff, B., Turkanis, C. G., & Bartlett, L. (2002). *Learning together: Children and adults in a school community*. Oxford, England: Oxford University Press.

Schunk, D. M., Pintrich, P. R., & Meece, J. L. (2008). *Motivation in education: Theory, research, and applications*. Upper Saddle River, NJ: Pearson Merrill/Prentice Hall.

Smith, A. (2014, January). African Americans and technology use: A demographic portrait. *Pew Research Center*. Retrieved from http://www.pewinternet.org/2014/01/06/african-americans-and-technology-use/

U.S. Department of Education. (2011a, November). *The potential impact of revising the Title I comparability requirement to focus on school-level expenditures*. Retrieved from https://www2.ed.gov/rschstat/eval/title-i/comparability-requirement/comparability-policy-brief.pdf

U.S. Department of Education. (2011b, November 30). *More than 40% of low-income schools don't get a fair share of state and local funds, Department of Education research*

finds [Press Release]. Retrieved from https://www.ed.gov/news/press-releases/
more-40-low-income-schools-dont-get-fair-share-state-and-local-funds-
department-education-research-finds
Zickuhr, K., & Smith, A. (2012, April 13). Digital differences. *Pew Research Center.*
Retrieved from http://www.pewinternet.org/2012/04/13/digital-differences/

CHAPTER 8

INTERACTIVE DIGITAL STORYBOOKS AND THE ROLE OF PARENTS IN SUPPORTING YOUNG CHILDREN'S MATHEMATICS DEVELOPMENT

Colleen Uscianowski, Ma. Victoria Almeda, and Herbert Ginsburg

Zoller, a fictional monster, invites three of her monster friends to come visit her music factory. "I can't wait to show you my Magnificent Monster Music factory," Zoller tells her friends, Marluk, Tigga, and Oona. "You won't believe my musical machines!" Tigga notices a large lever on the first machine: "Whoa, what's that big lever?" "Each machine has one. Pull the lever and watch as the musical instruments come bursting out," Zoller explains.

A set of drums comes bursting out of the machine, onto the conveyer belt. "I love musical instruments!" Marluk exclaims. Zoller tells the monsters, "You can help count and box them. How many drums do we have?"

A father is reading an interactive mathematics storybook called *Monster Music Factory* (*MMF*; Ginsburg, Cerf, & Creighan, 2016) with his 4-year-1-month-old son, Eddy.

Promising Practices for Engaging Families in STEM Learning, pp. 115–133
Copyright © 2018 by Information Age Publishing
115

Father: "You do, too [love musical instruments]" [gesturing to the instruments on display around his family's living room].

As Zoller tells her friends to help her count the number of drums, the father pauses the story and Eddy points to each drum, one at a time.

Son: "One, two, three, four, five."

Father: "Five drums! All right. You counted it before that monster!"

Interactive storybooks range in complexity, with little uniformity in format (Guernsey, Levine, Chiong, & Severns, 2012). Some contain few technological enhancements and resemble print books, but displayed on tablet devices. Others have many digital affordances, such as animation, sound effects, and games, which distinguish them from paper books. In this chapter, we focus on highly interactive storybooks (also called digital storybooks, electronic storybooks, or e-books) with various technological features.

MMF tells the story of Zoller Controller and her three monster friends as they help count, box, and deliver the musical instruments needed for a concert featuring the famous monster band, the Whirling Wailers. *MMF* operates on touch-screen tablet devices and each "page" of the storybook resembles a scene from a movie or play. The animated characters move and talk throughout the story as they demonstrate counting strategies and invite the child to engage with the characters and objects.

Our work investigates how adults in homes and preschools engage children in reading interactive storybooks, and how children learn mathematics in this context. The overall goal is to learn how to improve parent reading of interactive (and paper) storybooks and how to design effective storybooks. The target audience is preschool-aged children, especially those of underrepresented and low-income backgrounds, who often receive inferior education, at least in the United States (Ginsburg, Lee, & Boyd, 2008). Takacs, Swart, and Bus (2015) found that interactive storybook reading led to improved literacy outcomes among disadvantaged children who came from low socioeconomic status families, non-English speaking homes, or had learning disabilities. Interactive storybooks may thus be a beneficial learning tool for a diverse group of children.

We are particularly interested in studying the types of features that are realized with the help of technology and not possible in paper storybooks, such as animated characters and touch-screen capabilities, and how these features influence the child's mathematical learning. At the same time, we acknowledge that paper storybooks may possess beneficial features that interactive storybooks lack. We need to understand, improve, and promote the use of both.

In the first section of this chapter, we describe the unique affordances that reading on digital devices provide, such as immediate feedback. We then draw conclusions about effective interactive storybook reading practices. Finally, we describe our guide to reading *MMF*, which we created to help promote positive reading and mathematical interactions around this novel technology. Throughout, we illustrate the research with rich examples of Eddy reading *MMF* with his father.

AFFORDANCES AND LIMITATIONS OF DIGITAL FEATURES IN INTERACTIVE STORYBOOKS

Today's interactive storybooks present a variety of technological features that distinguish them from paper books (Bus, de Jong, & Verhallen, 2006).

Figure 8.1.   Counting drums for the Whirling Wailers.

Narrators read the text aloud as the words scroll along the bottom of the screen (see Figure 8.1). You can select words in the text and have the device read them aloud while an embedded dictionary provides its meaning. Children can click on objects in the illustration and bring them to life. Characters talk and walk across the screen and background objects make sound effects, such as the sound of a drumbeat as the drum is touched.

As interactive storybooks look increasingly less like their paper counterparts, questions arise: Can good interactive storybooks be as beneficial for learning as good paper books? Neither digital nor paper storybooks can guarantee success. Can the technological enhancements in interactive storybooks have negative effects, such as distracting children from understanding the plot? How can parents scaffold their children's learning when the story is embedded in technology and presented on a touch-screen device? The answers to these questions are crucial for storybook developers, and for the early childhood community, as we provide guidelines for parents around effective uses of interactive storybooks.

We believe that interactive storybooks *can be* a valuable learning tool – especially for mathematics—when two conditions are met: (1) when they are carefully designed with developmentally-appropriate digital features that do not overwhelm or distract the child; and (2) when the adult reads *with* the child and scaffolds learning by asking guiding questions and modeling good strategies, such as pausing the story to notice interesting mathematical concepts and connect the mathematics to the child's life. It is important for educators to evaluate and recognize high-quality, well-designed interactive storybooks, and to help guide parents in selecting and using them. Below we highlight three elements of well-designed interactive storybooks: animation and sound effects, touch screen capabilities, and immediate feedback.

Animation and Sound Effects

In the following scene of *MMF* (see Figure 8.2), the monsters count and pack the first instrument on their list: the tambourines. Eddy and his father share the story aloud.

Figure 8.2.   Tigga demonstrating how to count the tambourines.

Four tambourines squirt out of the machine. "I know, I know, I know! Three tambourines," Oona says excitedly.
The father pauses the story.

Father: "Are those three tambourines?" [Eddy touches each tambourine as he counts]

Son: "One, two, three, four."

Father: "Four tambourines!"

"Not so fast, Oona. Let's count them," Tigga suggests. Tigga touches each tambourine carefully, one at a time as he counts, "One, two, three, four! There are four tambourines altogether." Each time Tigga touches a tambourine, it shakes, makes a tambourine sound, lights up and stays lit as the other tambourines are touched. "Whoops, my bad. I should have counted," Oona laughs. "Push the number 4 on the machine," Zoller says.
Eddy pushes the number four and the tambourines drop into a four box.

Father: "What number was on the box?"

Son: "Four."

While images in a paper storybook remain static on the page, moving images in an interactive storybook have the ability to draw the child's attention to particular aspects of the scene and highlight relevant parts of the illustration (Bus, Takacs, & Kegel, 2015). The animation within each scene of *MMF* was created to demonstrate a different counting strategy. In the tambourines scene, the monsters demonstrate how to count carefully, with one-to-one correspondence. Tigga touches each tambourine slowly and one at a time. He also recites one number as he touches each tambourine, illustrating the counting principle that each object is assigned one and only one number word. When each tambourine is touched, it becomes animated: it shakes, makes a tambourine sound, and lights up. When Tigga says the number two, two tambourines glow and shake. This demonstrates the cardinal principle, or the idea that two does not only refer to the second tambourine, but to the entire set of two tambourines. The cardinal principle is reinforced with other sets of tambourines, as well.

Most research on interactive storybooks has focused on how they impact children's literacy skills (e.g., de Jong & Bus, 2004; Korat, 2010, Smeets & Bus, 2012). For example, Takacs et al. (2015) found that reading interactive storybooks was more beneficial than paper books for improving children's expressive vocabulary and story comprehension. Although research has not examined how interactive storybooks impact preschoolers' mathematical learning, studies have demonstrated that animated television shows can help reinforce young children's understanding of mathematical ideas (Anderson, Huston, Schmitt, Linebarger, & Wright, 2001; Fisch, 2004). In particular, the integration of animated visuals and sounds may be beneficial for helping young children comprehend the story and can help focus children's attention (Verhallen, Bus, & de Jong, 2006). Children process visual and verbal information in distinct channels, but when visual and verbal information are presented simultaneously, children are able to match the animation and sounds (Paivio, 1986). This leads to deeper understanding and better recall of the storybook content. However, the visual and verbal information must be closely related to one another and integral to the story in order to be effective for learning. Animation and sounds that draw the child's attention to irrelevant parts of the story that are incidental to the main plot can distract the child and disrupt comprehension (Bus et al., 2015).

Touch-Screen Capabilities

In the next scene of *MMF* (see Figure 8.3), the monsters count and pack the trumpets.

Figure 8.3. The monsters must decide how to count the messy pile of trumpets.

Tigga pulls the lever and a big burst of trumpets come out. The trumpets lay in a messy heap on the conveyer belt. "Whoa, that is a lot of trumpets. How are we going to count them all?" Marluk asks. "Don't worry, Marluk, we can just move them, one at a time, as we count them." Tigga slides a trumpet over as he counts, "One, two, three, four, five."

Eddy slides his finger along with Tigga, pushing the trumpets into a neat line on the conveyer belt as he counts them.

Interactive storybooks often contain "hotspots" that activate when touched. When Eddy touches the trumpets, he is able to slide them across the conveyer belt to line them up. Here the child is practicing another counting strategy, arranging the objects in an orderly way to help keep track of everything being counted. Eddy does not just watch Tigga slide the trumpets as he counts them, but he gets the opportunity to practice this strategy himself. Gestures are considered an important part of mathematical learning (Lakoff & Nunez, 2000), and interactive storybooks allow for children to gesture as they touch and manipulate objects on-screen. Research on mathematical software for preschool children suggests that manipulating digital objects can be at least as beneficial as manipulating physical objects (Clements & Sarama, 2007; Sarama & Clements, 2003). For example, Highfield and Mulligan (2007) compared children's ability to solve patterning tasks using physical materials and virtual tools, or manipulatives. They found that virtual tools afford the chance to create both a greater quantity and quality of patterns. Other studies suggest that virtual, on-screen manipulatives are easier to use and less distracting than their physical counterparts (Brown, McNeil, & Glenberg, 2009; Uttal, O'Doherty, Newline, Hand, & DeLoache, 2009). Digital storybooks that include games and hotspots provide the opportunity for children to manipulate on-screen objects, which helps add to the enjoyment of reading interactive storybooks (Moody, Justice, & Cabell, 2010). However, similar to animation and sound, hotspots and games should be congruent to the story's plot in order to support learning (Bus et al., 2015). Constantly switching between distracting hotspots and games, and then returning to the story, can disrupt the child's working memory and hinder learning (Mayer & Moreno, 2003).

Immediate Feedback

Appropriate feedback can have a robust effect on learning and motivation (Hattie & Timperley, 2007). Digital storybooks can be designed to provide specific, targeted feedback when a child makes a mistake, but not all feedback is effective. For example, Hattie (1999) suggests that the most constructive feedback is reinforcing, diagnostic, and goal-oriented, while ineffective feedback relies on extrinsic rewards and punishment. *MMF* was designed to provide productive feedback directly related to the goal of counting the number of instruments on each page. For instance, the first two times a child presses the wrong button to indicate the number of tambourines on the screen, Marluk says, "That's not how many tambourines there are. We should count again." Marluk is gently telling the child that his answer is incorrect, and he should try counting once more. If the child makes a subsequent mistake, Marluk provides even more support: "Hmmm. Maybe we should count them again. One … two. Try the two button." Marluk touches each tambourine as he counts, and the child can touch the tambourines and count along with him. Well-designed interactive storybooks respond to the child's incorrect responses by providing relevant feedback that guides the child to use appropriate strategies (Hirsh-Pasek et al., 2015). Interactive storybooks can also provide motivational messages (e.g., "Great job!") when the child solves a problem correctly. However, as Hattie (1999) warns, overreliance on extrinsic motivators and empty praise reduces task performance and decreases motivation.

In summary, because of their technological enhancements, reading interactive storybooks provides a different experience than does reading paper books. Given their affordances, interactive storybooks can enhance children's mathematical learning and provide many of the benefits of paper book reading. Animation and sound effects allow the characters in the story to model important mathematical concepts and principles that children can observe and imitate. In *MMF*, the monsters demonstrate how to count with one-to-one correspondence by touching each instrument once and only once as they recite the counting words. The cardinal principle is reinforced as the entire set of instruments glow, shake, and make sounds as the monsters, and then the children, count them. As the kazoos quickly fall from the chute, before children have the ability to count them individually, they must rely on their ability to subitize (i.e., instantly recognize the number of kazoos) in order to determine how many have fallen.

Touch-screen capabilities allow for children to try different counting strategies that the monsters demonstrate, such as pushing aside the trumpets one-by-one in order to keep track of them as they count. Children can learn to match a written numeral to the corresponding quantity of instruments by touching the buttons on the machine. If the child makes a mistake, the monsters provide immediate feedback by suggesting or demonstrating a constructive strategy, such as counting each instrument slowly and deliberately. However, interactive storybooks have the potential to hinder children's mathematical development if these types of technological enhancements are not congruent with the narrative, overwhelm working memory with distracting features, draw children's attention away from the central mathematical concepts and strategies, or rely on extrinsic motivators. Therefore, educators and parents must carefully review interactive storybooks and choose those with technological features that have the potential to foster children's foundational mathematical knowledge.

ENGAGING IN MEANINGFUL MATH CONVERSATIONS DURING STORYBOOK READING

One of the most important elements to promote mathematical learning through shared book reading is parents and children engaging in warm and rich mathematical conversations. In this section, we explore how families promote mathematical thinking through parent-child conversations during storybook reading and then describe a guide that we have developed to support parents in their efforts.

Mathematical conversations that take place between an adult and child during everyday activities impact how the child learns and thinks. For example, Pruden, Levine, and Huttenlocher (2011) studied parents' use of spatial language, such as words that describe the shapes and dimensions of objects. They found that the more parents provide their young children with spatial input during common activities, the more frequently do these children, at a later age, produce spatial words, and the better they perform on spatial problem-solving tasks.

Storybook reading is a type of common activity that is particularly conducive to immersing children in rich language and exposing them to new ideas. Literature on shared reading demonstrates that parents notice mathematical concepts in paper storybooks and engage their young children in conversations about the mathematics in the story (Anderson, Anderson, & Shapiro, 2005). In fact, children hear more diverse and complex language from storybook reading than from everyday talk (Montag, Jones, & Smith, 2015) or from conversations during meals, dressing, or play time (Hoff-Ginsberg, 1991). Storybooks embed ideas about number, size, shape, and spatial relations in the illustrations and text, using a narrative that is developmentally appropriate and engaging for young children.

Researchers have also investigated other effective ways of reading to children. Whitehurst created an interactive method of reading intended to promote children's language, thinking, and engagement (e.g., Zevenbergen & Whitehurst, 2003). This dialogic reading method guides the parent towards sharing the responsibility of being an active reader with the child, so that the child becomes a more engaged participant during reading. The parent can accomplish this by using open-ended prompts, repeating and expanding upon what the child is noticing, and using positive reinforcement.

When used effectively, dialogic reading can help children communicate about the story and improve their language skills (Sim, Berthelsen, Walker, Nicholson, & Fielding-Barnsley, 2014). Communication and language are key to mathematical learning (National Council of Teachers of Mathematics, 2000). Another consideration when reading with children is the level of complexity in the language parents use to ask questions and make comments about the story. Parents' use of more abstract, complex language during storybook reading is positively correlated with children's later abstract language abilities (van Kleeck, Gillam, Hamilton, & McGrath, 1997). Levels of complexity have been studied in the context of mathematical activities, as well. In a study of home learning activities, Skwarchuk (2009) found that children whose parents engage them in more complex number activities, such as adding or subtracting objects, achieved higher scores on a numeracy assessment. Conversely, children whose parents engaged them in more basic number activities, such as reciting numbers or reading printed numbers, achieved lower numeracy scores. We recommend that when reading storybooks, parents should ask a variety of questions, ranging from simpler to more complex. The father reading *MMF* with his son demonstrates this flexibility in questioning, as we saw earlier in the drum scene:

Father:	"Which button did the monster press?"	The father is asking a more basic question that requires the child to recall what just happened in the scene.
Son:	His son points to the five button: "Five."	
Father:	"Five. Why do you think he pressed five?"	This is a more complex question. The child needs to make an inference, understanding the connection between the written numeral 5 with the set of five drums.
Son:	[No answer]	His son doesn't answer, so the father asks a different question. The previous question may have been too complex, but the father skillfully scaffolds his son's understanding by asking a series of simpler questions.
Father:	"How many drums were there?"	
Son:	"Five."	
Father	"And where do they go?" Pointing to the five box.	
Son:	"In the box."	
Father:	"And what number's on the box?"	
Son:	"Five!"	
Father:	"Five drums. In a box that has a five."	Through asking a series of more basic questions, the father guided his child towards understanding why the monster pressed the five button.

In our own pilot studies, we have found that parents generally use more basic, simple questions when addressing mathematical content rather than literacy content in children's paper storybooks (Uscianowski, Almeda, Freeman, & Ginsburg, 2017). When primed to pose a question about character's actions or words, parents asked complex questions, requiring the child to identify similarities and differences or to predict what would happen next. In contrast, when primed about number or shape, parents asked simpler questions, such as labeling parts of an illustration or counting a small set of objects on the page. This suggests the need to educate parents to discuss mathematics in more complex ways with their children. To increase the complexity of math talk, parents can ask questions that encourage children to use inferencing or reasoning skills. For example, in addition to asking a child to count a small set of instruments, a parent might ask, "If two more instruments come out of the machine, how many instruments will there be?" or, "Why did Tigga press the 4 button just now?" Asking a mixture of simple questions, which build the child's confidence, and complex questions, which challenge the child, can lead to growth in mathematical knowledge.

THE GUIDE TO INTERACTIVE STORYBOOK READING FOR MONSTER MUSIC FACTORY

To help educate parents to engage in the practices described above we created a Guide to reading *MMF*, along with several other resources that reside on the tablet alongside the interactive storybooks. We did this because interactive storybooks with technological enhancements are a new type of technology that is just starting to become more commonplace in the home. Not only are many parents unfamiliar with interactive storybooks, they are also unfamiliar with research-tested methods of reading and with children's development of early mathematical knowledge.

We have also found that the parent's role is more varied and compli- cated in the context of interactive storybook reading than in reading paper books. Not only must the parent guide the child's understanding of the story elements, but the parent must also help the child navigate in a digital environment. In paper storybook reading, the reader controls the pace of the story. The reader decides when to pause and ask questions, when to move onto the next page, and when to turn back to a previous page to remember what happened earlier in the story. However, the role of the reader is more complex in interactive storybooks. Interactive storybooks often have a narrator who reads the story aloud to the child, and the story moves onto the next scene without the reader needing to turn a page. The reader may feel redundant, unsure what role to assume when reading technologically enhanced storybooks with a child.

Just as the parent should guide the child's learning by pausing to ask strategic questions and make interesting comments, the parent should also model appropriate use of technology. For example, in *MMF*, there are scenes where the monsters are modeling mathematical strategies that the child should observe before they are later given the chance to manipulate the instruments and practice various strategies themselves. In our obser- vations, children are eager to touch the characters and the background objects to animate them, but this detracts from their ability to focus on the narrative and attend to the mathematics in the story. The parent has the opportunity to remind the child when to watch the story unfold and when to count and box the instruments. Parents can also help young children, who may not have fully developed their fine motor skills, to gesture effectively on a touch-screen device. For example, in the tambourine scene, a parent might reinforce the technological capabilities by asking the child, "Did you see how Tigga slowly slid each trumpet into a line? Now it's your turn to carefully slide the trumpets, just like Tigga."

The Guide exists as a PDF document with embedded videos and illustrations and provides several different types of assistance. The purpose of the Guide is to provide parents with strategies on how and when to steer their children towards an enjoyable and stimulating reading experience that promotes mathematical learning. For example, in the drums scene described earlier, parents and children may not be aware of the opportune moments when the monsters are about to demonstrate an important strategy. The video demonstrations in the Guide may also be particularly useful for parents who are anxious about helping their children learn mathematics.

In the Guide, parents can watch embedded videos of specific scenes from *MMF*.

In the next episodes, the monsters try and figure out the number of instruments.

Zoller asks, "How many drums do we have?" Zoller pauses so that the child can count and then the drums levitate to allow your child to see exactly what Zoller is counting.

If your child starts counting faster or more slowly than Zoller, after she makes a slight pause, direct your child's attention: You can pause and say, "Remember is is Zoller's turn to count, so we can try counting with Zoller first." Then, press play. Point to each drum and count along with Zoller—"One, Two, Three, Four, Five!"

Figure 8.4.   The Guide shows Zoller counting the number of drums and suggests ways for the parent to engage the child.

Key features of the Guide include:

- A description of what is happening in each scene, along with the different ways in which a child may respond to each one. As shown in Figure 8.4, the Guide explains that there is a long pause before Zoller counts the number of drums on the conveyor belt, and children may get too excited and count faster than Zoller.

- When it is a monster's turn to count, parents should direct children's attention to what the monster is demonstrating or teaching them. In this case, by waiting for their turn to count, children may notice that the sounds that the drums make altogether represent the total number of drums.

- Access to embedded videos of parents who demonstrate important strategies for reading *MMF* to their children. As depicted in Figure 8.5, the Guide briefly describes the parent's strategy to help the child connect the number of drums in the box (cardinal number) to the written number depicted on the box (numeral). This connection is one of the important mathematical ideas of the drum scene.

In this video, the parent prompts the child to pay attention to the total number of drums by asking, "How many drums were there?" Afterwards, the parent asks, "What number is on the box?" This helps the child to notice that the total number of drums matches the number written on the box.

Figure 8.5.   The Guide shows a good example of a parent reading *Monster Music Factory*.

CONCLUSION

Recent studies suggest that interactive storybooks can have a stronger effect on vocabulary learning and reading comprehension than paper books or digital books without interactive enhancements (Smeets & Bus, 2015; Verhallen & Bus, 2010). We believe that the technological enhancements in interactive storybooks—such as animation, sounds, and touch-screen capabilities—can also help young children develop their mathematical knowledge and skills. In particular, we hope that our interactive mathematics storybooks will help disadvantaged children improve their numeracy skills, develop effective strategies for counting, and, most of all, enjoy mathematics and reading!

Key Takeaways

Help parents choose interactive storybooks wisely. The combination of animation and sounds make interactive storybooks a valuable learning tool. When selecting an interactive storybook to read with preschool children, ensure that animation is congruent with the sounds and narration. A close match between visual and verbal information will help promote learning and prevent overloading working memory. Interactive storybooks often incorporate features that allow for gesturing and touching on-screen objects, which can be particularly conducive for mathematical learning. If the games and hotspots are not relevant to the plot, they should come at the end, where they won't divert the child's attention away from the story.

We also recommend choosing digital storybooks that contain features allowing the parent and child to control the pace of the story. At a minimum, these features include a forward button, a backwards button, and a pause button. Parents can pause the story at key moments to ask questions and help the child decide when to press the forward button to move onto the next scene or backwards to reread a page. Although young children are becoming proficient at using technology, manipulating the interactive elements of the story may not be easy for them at the outset. Educators may have to help parents who have little familiarity with technology to become comfortable with and effectively use interactive storybooks.

Parents and caregivers matter. Parents facilitate their children's learning by engaging them in rich conversation, modeling good reading behaviors and mathematical strategies, and guiding their use of the digital device. Just as in paper storybook reading, parents should ask a variety of questions while reading interactive storybooks with their children. Incorporating mathematical language into these conversations can encourage young children to learn and use these important words. Building a strong early mathematical vocabulary not only boosts the child's understanding of mathematics, but also provides the means to communicate mathematical thinking and solve mathematical problems.

Have fun! When encouraging parents to read interactive storybooks with children, we in the early childhood community must remember that reading should be enjoyable. It should be a pleasurable activity and a magical opportunity for parents and children to bond over favorite stories. Interactive stories should be good pieces of literature that delight both children and their parents. In fact, research shows that reading interactive storybooks may be more engaging than paper books (Moody et al., 2010). As parents read storybooks, whether interactive or paper, they should look for opportunities to connect the story to the child's life. In encouraging interactive storybook reading, educators should always keep in mind the social-emotional and broader literacy context. We should not ruin a love of reading and an appreciation of good literature by choosing mediocre fiction or non-fiction mathematics storybooks that are didactic, boring, and pedestrian. Reading also provides the opportunity for the parent to connect and converse with the child, creating a warm environment supportive of early social-emotional growth. Put simply, mathematical content is not enough: interactive storybooks intended to teach mathematics must also have an intriguing plot, relatable characters, and beautiful illustrations. With these elements, interactive storybooks provide parents with valuable tools to teach children foundational mathematics knowledge.

REFERENCES

Anderson, A., Anderson, J., & Shapiro, J. (2005). Supporting multiple literacies: Parent's and children's mathematical talk. *Mathematics Education Research Journal, 16*(3), 5–26. doi:10.1007/BF03217399

Anderson, D. R., Huston, A. C., Schmitt, K. L., Linebarger, D. L., & Wright, J. C. (2001). Early childhood television viewing and adolescent behavior: The recontact study. *Monographs of the Society for Research in Child Development, 66*(1), 1–154. Retrieved from http://www.jstor.org/stable/3181552

Brown, M. C., McNeil, N. M., & Glenberg, A. M. (2009). Using concreteness in education: Real problems, potential solutions. *Child Development Perspectives, 3*(3), 160–164. doi:10.1111/j.1750-8606.2009.00098.x

Bus, A. G., de Jong, M. T., & Verhallen, M. (2006). CD-ROM talking books: A way to enhance early literacy? In M. C. McKenna, L. D. Labbo, R. D. Kiefer, & D. Reinking (Eds.), *International handbook of literacy and technology* (Vol II, pp. 129–142). Mahwah, NJ: Lawerence Erlbaum Associates.

Bus, A. G., Takacs, Z. K., & Kegel, C. A. T. (2015). Affordances and limitations of electronic storybooks for young children's emergent literacy. *Developmental Review, 35*, 79–97. doi:10.1016/j.dr.2014.12.004

Clements, D. H., & Sarama, J. (2007). Effects of a preschool mathematics curriculum: Summative research on the building blocks project. *Journal for Research in Mathematics Education, 38*(2), 136–163. Retrieved from https://www.du.edu/marsicoinstitute/media/documents/effectsofapreschoolmathematicscurric.pdf

de Jong, M., & Bus, A. G. (2004). The efficacy of electronic books in fostering kindergarten children's emergent story understanding. *Reading Research Quarterly, 39*(4), 378–393. doi:10.1598/RRQ.39.4.2

Fisch, S. M. (2004). *Children's learning from educational television: Sesame street and beyond.* Mahwah, NJ: Lawrence Erlbaum Associates.

Ginsburg, H. P., Cerf, C., & Creighan, S. (2016). *Monster Music Factory* (version 3.5.3) [application software]. Retrieved from https://www.speakaboos.com/story/monster-music-factory

Ginsburg, H. P., Lee, J. S, & Boyd, J. S. (2008). Mathematics education for young children: What it is and how to promote it. *Society for Research in Child Development Social Policy Report-Giving Child and Youth Development Knowledge Away, 22*(1), 1–24.

Guernsey, L., Levine, M., Chiong, C., & Severns, M. (2012). *Pioneering literacy in the digital Wild West: Empowering parents and educators.* New York, NY: The Joan Ganz Cooney Center at Sesame Street Workshop. Retrieved from http://joanganzcooneycenter.org/wp-content/uploads/2012/12/GLR_TechnologyGuide_final.pdf

Hattie, J. (1999). *Influences on student learning.* Inaugural professorial address. University of Auckland, New Zealand. Retrieved from https://cdn.auckland.ac.nz/assets/education/hattie/docs/influences-on-student-learning.pdf

Hattie, J., & Timperley, H. (2007). The power of feedback. *Review of Educational Research, 77*(1), 81–112. doi:10.3102/003465430298487

Highfield, K., & Mulligan, J. (2007). The role of dynamic interactive technological tools in preschooler's mathematical patterning. In J. Watson & K. Beswick (Eds.), *Proceedings of the 30th annual conference of the Mathematics Education Research Group of Australasia,* (Vol. 1, pp. 372–381). Sydney, Australia: MERGA, Inc. Retrieved from https://www.merga.net.au/documents/RP322007.pdf

Hirsh-Pasek, K., Zosh, J. M., Golinkoff, R. M., Gray, J. H., Robb, M. B., & Kaufman, J. (2015). Putting education in "Educational" apps: Lessons from the science of learning. *Psychological Science in the Public Interest, 16*(1), 3–34. doi:10.1177/1529100615569721

Hoff-Ginsberg, E. (1991). Mother-child conversation in different social classes and communicative settings. *Child Development, 62*(4), 782–796. doi:10.1111/j.1467-8624.1991.tb01569.x

Korat, O. (2010). Reading electronic books as a support for vocabulary, story comprehension and word reading in kindergarten and first grade. *Computers and Education, 55*(1), 24–31. doi:10.1016/j.compedu.2009.11.014

Lakoff, G., & Nunez, R. (2000). *Where mathematics comes from: How the embodied mind brings mathematics into being.* New York, NY: Basic Books.

Mayer, R. E., & Moreno, R. (2003). Nine ways to reduce cognitive load in multimedia learning. *Educational Psychologist, 38*(1), 43–52. doi:10.1207/S15326985EP3801_6

Montag, J. L., Jones, M. N., & Smith, L. B. (2015). The words children hear: Picture books and the statistics for language learning. *Psychological Science*, *26*(9), 1489–1496. doi:10.1177/0956797615594361

Moody, A. K., Justice, L. M., & Cabell, S. Q. (2010). Electronic versus traditional storybooks: Relative influence on preschool children's engagement and communication. *Journal of Early Childhood Literacy*, *10*(3), 294–313. doi:10.1177/1468798410372162

National Council of Teachers of Mathematics (NCTM). (2000). *Principles and standards for school mathematics*. Reston, VA: Author.

Paivio, A. (1986). *Mental representations: A dual coding approach*. Oxford, England: Oxford University Press.

Pruden, S. M., Levine, S. C., & Huttenlocher, J. (2011). Children's spatial thinking: Does talk about the spatial world matter? *Developmental Science*, *14*(6), 1417–1430. doi:10.1111/j.1467-7687.2011.01088.x

Sarama, J., & Clements, D. H. (2003). Building blocks of early childhood mathematics. *Teaching Children Mathematics*, *9*(8), 480–484. doi:10.1016/j.ecresq.2004.01.014

Sim, S. S. H., Berthelsen, D., Walker, S., Nicholson, J. M., & Fielding-Barnsley, R. (2014). A shared reading intervention with parents to enhance young children's early literacy skills. *Early Child Development and Care*, *184*(11), 1531–1549. doi:10.1080/03004430.2013.862532

Skwarchuk, S. (2009). How do parents support preschoolers' numeracy learning experiences at home? *Early Childhood Education Journal*, *37*(3), 189–197. doi:10.1007/s10643-009-0340-1

Smeets, D. J. H., & Bus, A. G. (2015). The interactive animated e-book as a word learning device for kindergartners. *Applied Psycholinguistics*, *36*(4), 899–920. doi:10.1017/S0142716413000556

Takacs, Z. K., Swart, E. K., & Bus, A. G. (2015). Benefits and pitfalls of multimedia and interactive features in technology-enhanced storybooks: A meta-analysis. *Review of Educational Research*, *85*(4), 698–739. doi:10.3102/0034654314566989

Uscianowski, C., Almeda, M. V., Freeman, C., & Ginsburg, H. (2017, April). *The relationship between level of abstraction and content in storybook reading*. In C. Lombardi & E. Dearing (Chairs), *Parent and early educator support of children's early mathematics learning*. Symposium conducted at the Society for Research in Child Development Biennial Meeting, Austin, TX.

Uttal, D. H., O'Doherty, K., Newland, R., Hand, L. L., & DeLoache, J. (2009). Dual representation and the linking of concrete and symbolic representations. *Child Development Perspectives*, *3*(3), 156–159. doi:10.1111/j.1750-8606.2009.00097.x

van Kleeck, A., Gillam, R. B., Hamilton, L., & McGrath, C. (1997). The relationship between middle-class parents' book-sharing discussion and their preschoolers' abstract language development. *Journal of Speech, Language, and Hearing Research*, *40*(6), 1261–1271. doi:10.1044/jslhr.4006.1261

Verhallen, M. J. A. J., & Bus, A. (2010). Low-income immigrant pupils learning vocabulary through digital picture storybooks. *Journal of Educational Psychology*, *102*, 54–61. doi:10.1037/a0017133

Verhallen, M. J. A. J., Bus, A. G., & de Jong, M. T. (2006). The promise of multimedia stories for kindergarten children at risk. *Journal of Educational Psychology*, *98*(2), 410–419. doi:http://dx.doi.org/10.1037/0022-0663.98.2.410

Zevenbergen, A. A., & Whitehurst, G. J. (2003). Dialogic reading: A shared picture book reading intervention for preschoolers. In A. van Kleeck, S. A. Stahl, & E. B. Bauer (Eds.), *Center for Improvement of Early Reading Achievement, CIERA. On reading books to children: Parents and teachers* (pp. 177–200). Mahwah, NJ: Lawrence Erlbaum Associates.

SECTION III

POLICIES SUPPORTING FAMILY
ENGAGEMENT IN STEM

Our final section focuses on how policies at the local, state, and federal level can support the promotion of family engagement in STEM. Policymakers have long been interested in STEM education as it is an important measure of our communities' and nation's economic growth and international standing. Policies with a strong family engagement and STEM focus create opportunities for equity in our society and a stronger likelihood that STEM initiatives will be sustained across time and place.

In Chapter 9, Andrés Henríquez describes a cross-systems local collaborative in Queens, New York spearheaded by the New York Hall of Science that offers immigrants and first-generation Americans a pathway out of poverty through a pipeline of STEM and career development programs. He also demonstrates how families' voices and feedback are shaping the core elements of this local initiative, including a Parent University designed to help parents increase their awareness of STEM career opportunities for their children.

In Chapter 10, Matthew Weyer examines why state-level policymakers should focus on early STEM and family engagement, and then explores state and federal actions that are bringing early STEM learning to the forefront of new and innovative policy. These include convening stakeholders to build STEM pathways from early childhood through high school, promoting high-quality curriculum and professional standards, and providing funding for the creation of innovative initiatives and programs.

In Chapter 11, Joan Walker looks at how the National Science Foundation supports family engagement in STEM learning. She provides examples of projects recently funded in four different project areas, and offers suggestions for researchers and practitioners who might be interested in applying for funding that supports family engagement in STEM programs and practices.

By concluding with a focus on policy it is our hope that families, schools, and communities will join together with policymakers to create new STEM investments with a strong focus on family engagement. The chapters in this section each end with key recommendations for making this a reality in local, state, and federal contexts.

CHAPTER 9

NYSCI NEIGHBORS

Creating Locally Driven Authentic Opportunities for Immigrant Parents in a STEM Ecosystem[1]

Andrés Henríquez

At a time when scientific and technological competence is vital to the nation's future, the underachievement of U.S. students in science in part reflects the uneven quality of science education. In New York City, for example, 62% of eighth grade students scored *below basic* level, 24% performed at the basic level, and only 13% scored at the *proficient* level on the Science portion of the National Assessment of Educational Progress, often referred to as our Nation's Report Card (National Center for Education Statistics, 2011). It has long been recognized that the level of pre-K–12 science, technology, engineering, and mathematics (STEM) education in the United States—particularly in poorer communities—is inadequate. For instance, a National Academy of Science report on minorities in STEM revealed that low-income families of color still do not have access to quality STEM education, which is linked to minorities' subsequent underrepresentation in STEM careers (Committee on Underrepresented Groups and the Expansion of the Science and Engineering Workforce Pipeline & Committee on Science, Engineering, and Public Policy and Global Affairs, 2011).

Promising Practices for Engaging Families in STEM Learning, pp. 137–146

The lack of STEM preparation among younger children from these communities—largely due to shortages in school resources, teacher professional development, and family engagement—undermines success in secondary school, college, and careers. STEM competencies—critical thinking, reasoning and argumentation, and metacognition—have been shown to be vital for success in the 21st century workplace (Committee on Underrepresented Groups and the Expansion of the Science and Engineering Workforce Pipeline & Committee on Science, Engineering, and Public Policy and Global Affairs, 2011); so remedying this situation is of great local and national importance.

In the fall of 2016, the New York Hall of Science (NYSCI) launched NYSCI Neighbors (formerly called Queens 20/20) to begin to address these concerns. NYSCI Neighbors creates an ecosystem for STEM learning by generating a model for broad and deep networks of STEM-rich opportunities in a high-need immigrant community in Queens, New York. Queens is often referred to as "the crossroads of the world," with a population of 2.3 million people, most of whom are immigrants. Through strategic partnerships with community organizations, local elected officials, schools, and education leaders, NYSCI Neighbors offers a multifaceted program of work that engages students, teachers, families, and community members in creative STEM learning.

In this chapter, we explore the inception of NYSCI Neighbors and the ways in which families' voices and feedback have shaped the core elements of this local initiative.

THE PROMISE OF LOCAL CROSS-INSTITUTIONAL COLLABORATIONS TO PROMOTE FAMILY ENGAGEMENT IN STEM

It is well established that STEM competencies are vital for success in the 21st century workplace. By 2022 there will be over 3 million job openings in STEM-related fields (Fayer, Lacey, & Watson, 2017). However, the quality of precollege STEM education in the United States—particularly in poorer communities—is inadequate. Low-income families of color still do not have access to quality STEM education and are underrepresented in science at every level (National Center for Science and Engineering Statistics, 2017).

In communities like Corona, Queens, these challenges are even more profound. Corona is in Community School District 24, one of the city's most crowded school districts, with 56 schools serving over 60,000 English language learners and Title 1 students. Additionally, 100% of local schools test below the state average in math and English language arts, and nearly all students are enrolled in free or reduced lunch programs. Corona is also a vibrant community with a bustling commercial hub populated by locally owned businesses, ethnic restaurants, cultural institutions and organizations, and is often a first stop for newly arrived immigrants. Nearly two-thirds of the community is foreign-born, and more than 90% speak a language other than English. Most residents are Latino—primarily from Ecuador, Colombia and Mexico, as well as other countries in Central and South America. Poverty rates in Corona are higher than in the rest of Queens, with more than 24% of households below the poverty line.

NYSCI Neighbors was developed as a hyperlocal initiative to offer immigrants and first-generation Americans a pathway out of poverty through a pipeline of STEM and career development programs. NYSCI Neighbors uses a multigenerational and multisystemic approach, providing multiple strategies and key programmatic interventions where both children and their caregivers are engaged as learners, and all the community stakeholders that have influence in a child's education are actively involved in their success and future outcomes. NYSCI Neighbors is a deep partnership among NYSCI, New York City's Community School District 24 (the largest school district in New York City), 20 schools and several neighborhood churches, libraries and community-based organizations. These institutions have joined together to provide out-of-school STEM opportunities, college preparation and career resources for youth, and programs that support parent engagement, learning, and leadership. A cornerstone of the initiative is the Science Ambassadors program, where students (pre-K to eighth grade) who attend any of the 20 local partner schools and their families are offered free admission and access to NYSCI's STEM exhibits, workshops, science and literacy programming, homework help, and more at the museum during the critical hours of 2 P.M.–5 P.M. during the school year.

But why would a museum serve as the anchor institution of a community initiative to tackle these gaps? First, museums like NYSCI provide degrees of freedom for children and families to learn in an environment without the pressures of accountability. NYSCI is deeply committed to *design, make, play* philosophy. DESIGN means there are problems worth solving that can give young people both purpose and agency as well as being able to understand that there are divergent solutions to a problem. MAKE allows youngster to use real materials, think with their hands, and build things while building skills. PLAY promotes the intrinsic motivation, deep engagement, and delight that will encourage children to maintain their involvement in STEM learning.

Second, NYSCI is a warm and inviting space to be in. It is a premier science center with cutting edge exhibits, a maker space, learning labs, and a science and technology library. It also has a program team of PhD level learning scientists *and* practitioners focused on innovative approaches to intergenerational STEM learning. NYSCI has emerged as a trusted community space through years of relationship-building; this is reflected in the initiative's advisory board, a local advisory council representing educators, school-based parent coordinators, parents, and members of non-profit organizations and churches. To ensure that the NYSCI Neighbors is educationally and culturally appropriate, NYSCI also has a national advisory board of individuals with expertise in English language learners, computer science, and youth development experts.

ENGAGING FAMILIES IN STEM ECOSYSTEMS

Perhaps one of the most important aspects of NYSCI Neighbors is its goal to promote parent, family, and community engagement. Parental support in taking children to informal learning institutions (libraries, museums) and STEM relevant afterschool programs has been shown to have a positive effect on children's participation in math and science activities in general (Simpkins, Davis-Kean, & Eccles, 2005). Studies have also shown that parents who convey the importance of STEM subjects motivate their children to take more science and math courses (Harackiewicz, Rozek, Hulleman, & Hyde, 2012; Rozek, Hyde, Svoboda, Hulleman, & Harackiewicz, 2015). Furthermore, research suggests that family engagement for young people of all ages yields positive results: children stay in school longer, perform better in school, and generally have better school experiences. This is consistent across grade levels in both formal and informal school contexts (Henderson & Mapp, 2002; Jeynes, 2005; Lopez & Caspe, 2014). Parent engagement in STEM, particularly for those with underserved young children, has a powerful effect on children's learning. When given more direction, parents from diverse backgrounds can become more engaged with their children—and when parents are more engaged, children tend to do better in STEM (National Science Teacher Association, 2009; Van Voorhis, Maier, Epstein, & Lloyd, 2013).

Yet, research suggests that immigrant parents face challenges in facilitating their children's STEM learning. Parents with children who are English language learners have double the amount of work: having to learn both English and the language of science and mathematics (Short & Fitzsimmons, 2007). Even though parents see themselves as important to inspiring their children's interest in STEM learning, almost a third do not feel comfortable in their own STEM knowledge to adequately support academic and career goals for their children (Jackson & King, 2016).

For years, parent engagement has focused on parents advocating for their children in school. Parents who are newcomers to this country may receive support, but it is often focused on immigrant rights and advocacy. Improving child outcomes depends on supporting families in gaining access to guidance and support on a range of issues. In *Children of Immigration*, Suarez-Orazco and Suarez-Orozco (2001) identified a split between aspirations and actual choices that grows over time as children encounter obstacles. NYSCI's work is intended to address this split in such a way that aspiration and choice are effectively coupled, and parents and their children have the knowledge and opportunities required to succeed in STEM fields both academically and professionally.

RAISING FAMILIES' VOICES

In order to elevate families' perspectives to improve the initiative and services offered, NYSCI Neighbors engaged in a number of activities to listen and learn from families. The goal of this outreach was to answer several questions:

- How do parents perceive their children vis-à-vis STEM?
- What are children's access to STEM-rich opportunities in school? Out of school?
- How do parents navigate the transitions from one school to another (i.e., elementary to middle and middle to high school)?
- How are parent groups engaging parents in their child's STEM education?

First, NYSCI Neighbors held two focus groups with parents at NYSCI; parents were recruited from local schools, and there were 10 parents in each group. Each focus group lasted 45 minutes and was conducted in both Spanish and English. The overall goal of the focus groups was to learn parents' perspectives of their children's career aspirations vis-à-vis their future role in the STEM workforce.

NYSCI Neighbors staff also conducted interviews with a number of stakeholders involved in family and community engagement: the district superintendent, assistant superintendent, the district's director of parent coordinators, the New York City Department of Education family and community engagement staff, and a number of math and science teachers. The purpose of these interviews was to better understand and build on parent engagement efforts taking place in the school district.

Finally, NYSCI Neighbors did an informal landscape analysis that reviewed existing local and national parent engagement resources and platforms. Staff used this analysis to get a better understanding of some of the local and national efforts in parent engagement and STEM. To conduct the analysis, NYSCI staff met with the main Queens Public Library staff, as well as with local Corona librarians to explore parent engagement strategies. Staff also had discussions with national providers, including Learning Leaders, Parent Institute for Quality Education members, Home Instruction for Parents of Preschool Youngsters personnel, and Learning Heroes staff. Among the resources explored in the landscape analysis was the comprehensive national parent survey, *Parents 2016: Hearts and Minds of Parents in an Uncertain World*, surveying 1,200 parents of children from kindergarten through eighth grade (Learning Heroes, 2016). The report showed that top concerns of Latino parents include financing college and children's social and emotional health and safety. Staff used this report to see how our local effort would compare to a national representative sample.

Three main themes emerged from the focus groups, interviews, and landscape analysis.

- **Parents are committed to helping students achieve their STEM goals but want to know how to help with actionable steps.** Families want their aspirations for their children to be validated, and they desire knowledge about specific steps to help them realize their child's ambitions. Families want to be in the driver's seat and learn how to support their children in STEM learning and academics in general. And this means they need information that empowers them to be effective role models and to understand middle, high school, and college access. One parent, Sylvia Sanchez[2]—a Community Advisor, PTA president, and a parent of two young children attending schools in District 24—expressed what many parents have conveyed to NYSCI: Sylvia wants her children to feel motivated by what is possible—becoming an astronaut or engineer—but she also wants those dreams to be *attainable*. As a parent, she is absolutely committed to helping her children achieve their goals and aspirations, but she wants to know how to best support them with actionable steps.
- **Parents want a place for the entire family where their culture is valued.** Parents want a place that is comfortable and accessible, where they can learn and have fun with their children, and interact with people who speak their native language. They want a place where the *entire* family is welcome—multigeneration and multi-caretaker families are common in this community. And they want to feel informed about the educational value of what their children are doing (e.g., connections to STEM subject matter, and to learning skills like problem solving, teamwork, and critical thinking); and to know how science is connected to their cultural traditions and practices.
- **Parents often feel disconnected from schools.** It was clear from the focus group data that immigrant parents feel disconnected

from school. Additionally, the focus groups revealed that these parents feel too intimidated to ask questions about their children's future and trajectory. What's more, parents find it difficult to understand how to navigate a complex school system for their children, specifically when it comes to STEM education and STEM-themed schools.

PARENT UNIVERSITY: DESIGNING NEW SERVICES BASED ON FAMILIES' NEEDS

A direct outgrowth of the focus group interviews with families and educators was the development of NYSCI's Parent University. The goal of Parent University is to help parents increase their awareness of STEM career opportunities for their children, and to offer the tools and resources needed to help their children achieve academic and career success. Parent University uses a variety of strategies to engage parents to meet this goal. The program provides parents with tools and resources to help them understand and navigate the school system in New York, throughout the continuum of their child's education (pre-K to college). It increases parents' awareness and access to essential STEM academic coursework and real pathways to STEM-related careers. It also emphasizes a two-generation approach—for children AND families—to provide STEM programs that privilege creativity and hands-on exploration. Parent University offers activities across multiple settings with parents, parent associations, Community School District 24, and other community members to foster student success and learning as a shared responsibility. It also gives local immigrant parents and families a voice and a platform to ensure their concerns, challenges, and stories are recognized throughout the district, city, and nation.

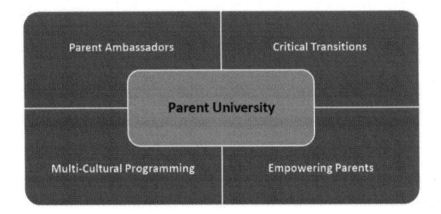

Figure 9.1.   NYSCI Neighbors Parent Univeristy Framework.

The Parent University framework includes:

1. **A parent ambassadors program.** Through this program, parents have the opportunity to learn about STEM concepts in a hands-on science center environment and grow as leaders and STEM advocates in their community.
2. **A focus on critical school transitions.** The program is producing resources that will help families navigate critical school transitions and opportunities available in STEM-focused high schools, colleges, and careers in linguistically and culturally attuned settings.
3. **Parent empowerment opportunities.** The program empowers parents by offering courses and opportunities in collaboration with partners like New York City's Department of Education's Adult and Continuing Education program to engage them as learners and increase their understanding of how science can help them make informed decisions for their families.
4. **Multicultural programming.** By focusing on families' culture and strengths, families see NYSCI as a place for them, one that honors STEM in diverse cultural contexts.

KEY IMPLICATIONS

As NYSCI Neighbors grows in size and reach, we anticipate additional positive learning impacts. For others interested in creating similar local, community-wide initiatives, we recommend the following:

- **Develop partnerships to augment impact.** On their own neither families, schools, or community institutions will ensure young people reach their full STEM potential. Instead, it takes a cross-sector collaborative where schools, community-based organizations, and all local institutions work together to get families and children engaged. An old axiom reminds us that the sum is greater than its parts.
- **Build initiatives and programs with parents' ideas and voices at the forefront**. By collecting data from focus groups, interviews, and landscape analysis, the NYSCI Neighbors initiative has been able to place families' interests and needs at the forefront of services. The development of Parent University is a direct outgrowth of parents' desire to learn how to navigate their local school system and help their children reach their STEM goals.

NOTES

1. An earlier version of this chapter appeared in the proceedings of the NSF INCLUDES Conference, Advancing the Collective Impact of Retention and Continuation Strategies for Hispanics and other Underrepresented Minorities in STEM Fields, March 2017. Support for Parent University was provided by Carnegie Corporation of New York and the Deutsche Bank Americas Foundation.
2. Sylvia Sanchez's name is an alias.

REFERENCES

Committee on Underrepresented Groups and the Expansion of the Science and Engineering Workforce Pipeline & Committee on Science, Engineering, and Public Policy and Global Affairs. (2011). *Expanding underrepresented minority participation*. Washington, DC: National Academies Press. Retrieved from https://grants.nih.gov/training/minority_participation.pdf

Fayer, S., Lacey, A., & Watson, A. (2017). *BLS spotlight on statistics: STEM occupations past, present, and future*. Washington, DC: U.S. Department of Labor, Bureau of Labor Statistics.

Harackiewicz, J. M., Rozek, C. S., Hulleman, C. S., & Hyde, J. S. (2012). Helping parents to motivate adolescents in mathematics and science an experimental test of a utility-value intervention. *Psychological Science, 23*(8), 899–906. doi:https://doi.org/10.1177/0956797611435530

Henderson, A. T., & Mapp, K. L. (2002). *A new wave of evidence: The impact of school, family, and community connections on student achievement* [Annual Synthesis 2002]. Austin, TX: National Center for Family and Community Connections with Schools. Retrieved from https://www.sedl.org/connections/resources/evidence.pdf

Jackson, R., & King, M. P. (2016). *Increasing student's access to opportunities in STEM by effectively engaging families*. Alexandria, VA: National PTA. Retrieved from http://s3.amazonaws.com/rdcms-pta/files/production/public/Images/STEM_Whitepaper_FINAL.pdf

Jeynes, W. H. (2005). A meta-analysis of the relation of parental involvement to urban elementary school student academic achievement. *Urban Education, 40*(3), 237–269. doi:https://doi.org/10.1177/0042085905274540

Learning Heroes. (2016). *Parents 2016: Hearts & minds of parents in an uncertain world*. Retrieved from https://r50gh2ss1ic2mww8s3uvjvq1-wpengine.netdna-ssl.com/wp-content/uploads/2017/04/LearningHeroes-Report-english.pdf

Lopez, M. E., & Caspe, M. (2014). *Family engagement in anywhere, anytime learning*. Cambridge, MA: Harvard Family Research Project. Retrieved from http://engagefamilies.org/wp-content/uploads/2017/04/HFRP-Family-Engagement-in-Anywhere-Anytime-Learning-2014-1.pdf

National Center for Education Statistics. (2011). *The nation's report card: Trial urban district assessment science 2009* (NCES 2011-452). Washington, DC: Institute of Education Sciences, U.S. Department of Education, Retrieved from https://nces.ed.gov/nationsreportcard/pdf/dst2009/2011452.pdf

National Center for Science and Engineering Statistics. (2017). *Women, minorities, and persons with disabilities in science and engineering: 2017* [Special Report NSF 17-310]. Arlington, VA: National Science Foundation. Retrieved from www.nsf.gov/statistics/wmpd/

National Science Teacher Association. (2009). *NSTA position statement: Parent involvement in science learning*. Arlington, VA: National Science Teacher Association. Retrieved from http://static.nsta.org/pdfs/PositionStatement_ParentInvolvement.pdf

Rozek, C. S., Hyde, J. S., Svoboda, R. C., Hulleman, C. S., & Harackiewicz, J. M. (2015). Gender differences in the effects of a utility-value intervention to help parents motivate adolescents in mathematics and science. *Journal of Educational Psychology, 107*(1), 195–206.

Short, D., & Fitzsimmons, S. (2007). *Double the work: Challenges and solutions to acquiring language and academic literacy for adolescent English language learners*. Washington, DC: Alliance for Excellent Education. Retrieved from https://www.carnegie.org/media/filer_public/bd/d8/bdd80ac7-fb48-4b97-b082-df8c49320acb/ccny_report_2007_double.pdf

Simpkins, S. D., Davis-Kean, P. E., & Eccles, J. S. (2005). Parents' socializing behavior and children's participation in math, science, and computer out-of-school- activities. *Applied Developmental Science, 9*(1), 14–30. doi:http://dx.doi.org/10.1207/s1532480xads0901_3

Suarez-Orozco, C., & Suarez-Orozco, M. (2001). *Children of immigration*. Cambridge, MA: Harvard College Press.

Van Voorhis, F. L., Maier, M. F., Epstein, J. L., & Lloyd, C. M. (2013). *The impact of family involvement on the education of young children 3 to 8: A focus on literacy and math achievement outcomes and social-emotional skills*. New York, NY: MDRC. Retrieved from https://www.mdrc.org/sites/default/files/The_Impact_of_Family_Involvement_FR.pdf

CHAPTER 10

POLICY SUPPORTS FOR FAMILY ENGAGEMENT IN EARLY STEM

Matthew Weyer

Science, technology, engineering, and mathematics (STEM) education is vital to our nation's global competitiveness, economic growth, and overall standard of living. For this reason, education and economic policy reform has increasingly focused on STEM-related issues —from filling workforce needs to improving mathematics and science skills for all children from preschool through high school. A policy emphasis on supporting STEM skills in the early years is particularly important because a strong STEM foundation sets the stage for future STEM learning. Policy efforts to promote early STEM also help direct attention and resources to a period in which STEM skills are often given a backseat to literacy skills and social-emotional learning. Because families are children's first teachers and their biggest advocates, policy reform also requires attention to the role of family engagement in early STEM learning.

The goal of this chapter is to underscore the importance of STEM education in the early years and to explore how policies at the federal and state levels can effectively promote both early STEM and families' engagement in children's early STEM learning. The chapter begins with an overview of why policymakers should focus on early STEM and family engagement,

Promising Practices for Engaging Families in STEM Learning, pp. 147–160
Copyright © 2018 by Information Age Publishing

and then explores state and federal actions that are bringing early STEM learning to the forefront of new and innovative policy.

WHY SHOULD POLICY FOCUS ON FAMILY ENGAGEMENT AND EARLY STEM?

Policy efforts are focusing on family engagement and early STEM for four main reasons—(1) family engagement in STEM learning is important for children's educational outcomes; (2) STEM success is an important component of building societal equity; (3) STEM competence is a global and economic imperative, and (4) families desire greater engagement.

THE SHORT- AND LONG-TERM EDUCATIONAL IMPORTANCE OF EARLY STEM

When young children enter school, they already have substantial knowledge of the natural world, can think both concretely and abstractly, use a range of scientific reasoning processes, and are eager, curious and ready to learn (Amsterlaw & Wellman, 2006; Tytler & Peterson, 2003). Even infants can reason, problem solve, and test physical hypotheses by observing objects behaving in unexpected ways (Gopnik, Meltzoff, & Kuhl, 2000; Stahl & Feigenson, 2015; Woodward, 2009).

Strengthening these innate abilities can begin during infancy and continue throughout early childhood, and both classroom and home experiences can serve as charging stations to amplify these skills (Phillips et al., 2017). For example, children's mathematical skills in preschool are correlated to the number of mathematical words that young children are exposed to in the home between 14 and 30 months of age (Levine, Suriyakham, Rowe, Huttenlocher, & Gunderson, 2010). Similar research has also demonstrated that parents' use of spatial words with young children is correlated with later spatial thinking ability, a critical STEM skill (Pruden, Levine, & Huttenlocher, 2011). High quality preschools are a means to sustain these gains and set students up on positive academic trajectories (see Dodge, Bai, Ladd, & Muschkin, 2016; Huang, 2017; Lipsey, Farran, & Hofer, 2015; Phillips, Gormely, & Anderson, 2016).

Developing STEM skills early can also help long-term achievement. Early mathematical skills are the strongest predictor of academic achievement at age 15 (Duncan et al., 2007; Watts, Duncan, Siegler, & Davis-Kean, 2014). Valuing and emphasizing early STEM skills might also begin to reverse decades-old trends of low mathematics and science achievement in the United States. For example, in 2009, only 39% of the nation's fourth graders scored at or above proficiency in mathematics; in 2015, this score only increased by one percentage point (National Assessment of Educational Progress, 2015).

THE URGENT DEMAND TO MEET THE NEEDS OF UNDERSERVED POPULATIONS

Underserved students (those from low-income families and/or children of color) as young as age 4 have been shown to have significant gaps in their science knowledge as compared to their White and middle- and high-income peers; these gaps also tend to persist across these students' careers, from kindergarten through grade 12 (K–12; Morgan, Farkas, Hillemeier, & Maczuga, 2016). Students from low-income households are also markedly behind their higher-income peers in mathematics (Jordan, Kaplan, Oláh, & Locuniak, 2006). Families can and have worked to reverse this trend; recent research has demonstrated that increased family engagement has contributed to lessening the gap (Bassok & Latham, 2017; Reardon & Portilla, 2016).

Deficits in early mathematics and science achievement for low-income students can be attributed both to a lack of opportunities and to gaps in access to highly qualified teachers, resources (e.g., curricula and technology), and after school opportunities. Discussing supplemental STEM programming at the high school level, Gottfried and Williams (2013) have suggested that, "low-income communities and schools may have fewer activities available and fewer high quality resources (i.e., teachers) to support these activities even if they were present" (p. 19). Providing more high quality early learning opportunities in STEM subjects holds positive implications for low-income students' achievement.

Low-income and students of color are not the only underserved populations in need of a renewed focus on early STEM education. English learners (ELs) make up significant portions of the K–12 population in many states (Ruiz Soto, Hooker, & Batalova, 2015) and are a valuable, often underutilized resource in developing state economies. Within the larger group of ELs, dual language learners (DLLs) are students whose native language is not English and who are simultaneously learning their second language (English) while mastering their native language. DLLs are the youngest portion of the larger spectrum of the group of ELs, generally classified as birth through age eight. In 2012, these students comprised nearly 30% of all Head Start and Early Head Start students (Aikens, Atkins-Burnett, & Bandel, 2012). In 2008, K–12 aged DLL/ELs represented one in nine students; by 2028 this number is expected to reach one in four (Goldenberg, 2008). From 2004 to 2014, several states experienced rapid growth of their

EL populations, especially in the southeast: South Carolina (236%), Maryland (180%), Mississippi (131%), Arkansas (102%), and Kentucky (98%; U.S. Department of Education, 2016).

THE ECONOMIC AND
GLOBAL COMPETITIVENESS IMPERATIVE

Developing STEM knowledge and skills among our youngest learners is also an economic imperative in the United States. Many STEM jobs remain unfilled (New American Economy, 2017), and are projected to be increasingly in demand, with this sector growing by 17% from 2008–2018, compared to 9.8% for all other occupations (Langdon, McKittrick, Beede, Khan, & Doms, 2011). Computer science and information technology jobs are expected to increase the fastest among all occupations, adding approximately 488,500 new jobs between 2014 and 2024 (Bureau of Labor Statistics, 2015). Additionally, STEM workers are more likely to earn higher wages than their non-STEM counterparts (Carnevale et al., 2011). Improving early STEM education can systemically address this workforce shortage and leverage U.S. workers to take advantage of growth in the STEM sector.

Internationally, the U.S. is falling behind its top counterparts in science and mathematical achievement. This reduces our global competitiveness and diminishes the many economic and societal benefits derived from having a highly skilled STEM workforce (Belfali & Ikeda, 2016). Having a pool of qualified candidates is a critical need in every state, and begins with a strong foundational education in STEM knowledge and skills. Currently, 64% and 59% of high school graduates are not academically ready for college-level science and mathematics, respectively (ACT, 2017). U.S. students' performance in mathematics and science has fallen significantly since 2000, when they ranked 19th, to 2012, when they ranked 36th. In science, the U.S. ranked 14th in 2000 and fell to 25th in 2016 (Schleicher, 2016; Schleicher & Davidson, 2012). Building systemic and purposeful policies for developing STEM skills at a young age could have tremendous benefits for our nation's economic future, global competitiveness, security, and well-being.

THE ESSENTIAL ROLE OF FAMILIES IN STEM LEARNING

Family engagement refers to the conscious effort on the part of parents, caregivers, and other family members (e.g., legal guardians, older siblings) to engage in a child's education and development by promoting positive behaviors at home and ensuring that children go to school ready to learn. From birth, children are already engaging with their parents and families in STEM-like activities. However, parents sometimes lack confidence in their ability to support STEM learning (see Chapter 4, this volume): 46% of parents said they play the biggest role in stimulating their child's interest in science, ahead of teachers (44%), yet 31% of parents don't feel comfortable enough in their scientific knowledge to help their children engage in hands-on science activities (Bayer Corporation, 2015).

Parents also hold implicit expectations and beliefs regarding gender differences in STEM abilities. For example, when visiting a museum, parents are three times more likely to explain science exhibits to their boys than to their girls (Crowley, Callanan, Tenenbaum, & Allen, 2001). Implicit biases and assumptions such as this can negatively impact parent-child engagement and subsequent learning. Even high-achieving girls and women have low levels of confidence in their ability to solve science and mathematical problems (Organization for Economic Co-operation and Development, 2015). Although low levels of confidence likely result from a combination of factors (e.g., parental bias, societal expectations), there still is a clear impact on STEM education achievement and attainment that must be addressed.

In response to parental expressions of anxiety and/or their lack of awareness of the importance of early STEM development, advocacy groups have suggested that parents need to develop their confidence and efficacy as their children's STEM "guides" (McClure et al., 2017). Parents must also become informed and powerful advocates for their children (Bowman et al., 2017). To do so, parents need concise and accurate research summaries, and concrete ideas for supporting early STEM education. Early STEM advocates can support parents through outreach, websites, community engagement, public service announcements, and marketing. Parents can be instrumental in addressing any anxieties or misconceptions their children (or they) have around STEM skills—that they are innate, that girls are not good at STEM, or any other public perceptions that negatively impact STEM skill development. Moreover, parents and families are important champions to move policy and reform movements forward, but need guidance on how to do so.

CURRENT POLICY EFFORTS PROMOTING FAMILY ENGAGEMENT AND EARLY STEM

The following section explores state and federal actions promoting family engagement in early STEM. States are promoting family engagement in early STEM in a variety of ways: by convening leadership bodies, setting high standards, promoting high-quality curriculum and professional development, and funding innovative programs. The federal government is also providing support for family engagement in early STEM through a variety of programs and policies.

STATE-LEVEL STEM PROMOTION

Convening Stakeholders to Build STEM Pathways From Early Childhood Through High School

In recent years, several state legislatures have created STEM advisory councils (under the jurisdiction of the state executive branch) that serve to organize and govern future efforts to study and improve upon the continuum of STEM education from preschool through grade 12. These councils generally report to the legislature and governor on accountability outcomes to ensure continued funding, and are comprised of leaders from higher education, the private sector, preschool and K–12 educators, and state and local government officials.

States are also forming teams to work together to create legislation that supports STEM and early learning. In a comprehensive state policy scan, 49 early STEM education bills were introduced from 2015–2017, and of those introduced, 27 were enacted. Most legislation funded the development of new programs, such as STEM centers, the development of curricula and standards, professional development for teachers, and the initiation or renewal of grant programs to fund STEM endeavors. Although none of these enacted bills explicitly mentions family engagement, it is in many cases an implicit element for bills focusing on developing preschool and elementary STEM education. For instance, Colorado has enacted legislation creating a seal of STEM proficiency for graduating high school seniors, denoting a high level of proficiency in STEM education and affixed to the honoree's high school diploma. The legislation encourages students and their parents to start thinking about the seal process early.

Regulations and best practices may help move the creation of this STEM pathway even earlier, potentially beginning in preschool. For example, preschoolers could be informally assessed in STEM subjects in a developmentally-appropriate manner by both families and teachers through observations of play or performance-based objectives. Later, third graders could demonstrate their STEM proficiency with an in-depth science project completed at home and school. Both assessments would serve as benchmarks in students' preschool to grade 12 STEM learning, perhaps culminating in a STEM seal. Focusing on pathways also allows for early identification of struggling students in these areas, as well as development of age-appropriate interventions to get students back on track.

A handful of state legislators also have been actively introducing legislation aimed at increasing the participation of women/girls and underrepresented groups in STEM education. These bills aim to increase awareness and interest, provide financial assistance (e.g., for improving broadband access, equipment, technology, and facility use) and require evaluative mechanisms (i.e. reporting) to make sure they are having a positive impact.

Cumulatively, these state-level efforts demonstrate the importance of STEM education beginning in the early years, and providing professional development for educators as well as incentives for STEM-focused careers. However, there remains a need for more legislative champions willing to be pioneers, build consensus, and craft legislation, with a particular eye toward engaging families in these initiatives.

Promoting High-Quality Curriculum and Professional Development and Setting Standards

States have also begun to take the lead in developing standards, curriculum, and professional development efforts to promote high-quality STEM education, with strong family engagement efforts as a central component. For example, the Iowa Ramps & Pathways Project, funded by the National Science Foundation, is a university-based program that provides professional development and training to preschool through second grade teachers across the state to nurture engineering habits of mind in children and to help students learn the laws of physics. This classroom-tested curriculum not only increased preschool through second graders' science achievement, but also enhanced teachers' confidence in their abilities to teach science to young children.

Another program of note, the New Mexico STEM-H Connection, is a statewide collaborative effort to promote STEM (plus health) education in homes throughout New Mexico. STEM-H's online platform provides a robust database of programming for parents and teachers to engage their children and students in STEM-H activities. The online platform also serves as a link to connect community volunteer experts to teach students in these areas.

Researchers have also proposed expanding the family-school partnerships standards set by the National Parent Teacher Association (PTA) from one-time, add-on events to a more systemic, integrated, and continuous method of engaging families in the STEM disciplines (Jackson & King, 2016). Many examples of effective STEM programs exist across the country, ranging from supplemental programs at community libraries, to in-depth, university-based summer camps, to Internet-based supports for at-home learning, yet nearly none have explicit family engagement standards. The National PTA standards could be adapted to include: welcoming families and encouraging their involvement, promoting two-way communication between teachers and parents, informing parents of the value of developing early STEM skills, and helping them advocate for their children, among other engagement efforts.

Providing Funding for the Creation of Innovative Initiatives and Programs

States are also developing innovative programs. The following are examples of programs designed and funded through state legislation that are enabling effective early STEM education and providing resources and opportunities for parents to engage in the programs.

Michigan. The Michigan STEM Partnership coordinates all state efforts in STEM education. Utilizing a hub model, the partnership connects schools and teachers with STEM providers and partners to create STEM educational programming and job training. Their online platform provides a series of resources for parents, including links to STEM programs for children and links to STEM-related degrees, occupations, and data.

Minnesota. The Headwaters Science Center has provided intellectually stimulating science programming for kids (and parents) since 1993. A central feature of engaging families is Science Saturdays, which feature presentations from local STEM professionals that engage children and their families in STEM-based activities. This program serves hundreds of families each year and provides a forum for collaboration and learning.

Virginia. In 2015, the Virginia General Assembly appropriated funding for five public school districts to support implementation of a STEM model program for preschool and kindergarten students. This appropriation focused on developing STEM skills through integration of the arts; it also appropriated funding to provide mathematics specialists for underperforming schools.

It should be explicitly noted that funding for these state-level programs varies greatly. Some programs are line-item budgets in legislation, some are privately funded, and others are a combination of multiple funding sources, created through a braiding of funds. The two most critical funding elements for STEM programs are that they ensure high quality programming and outcomes and that they are sustainable. Without adequate funding for high quality, early STEM programs are unlikely to produce their intended outcomes and, in some cases, may even be detrimental to student learning. Sustainability is also a critical element, as programs that are available on a seemingly random basis may prove ineffective in consistently enrolling students, engaging parents, and demonstrating sustained impact over time.

FEDERAL-LEVEL STEM PROMOTION

As discussed by Walker in this volume (Chapter 10), ongoing efforts exist to enhance STEM learning opportunities for students and families in programs across the country. Further, the STEM Education Act of 2015 expanded research and training opportunities for mathematics and science teachers, boosted informal STEM research, and explicitly incorporated computer science into the definition of STEM education. Additionally, the Early STEM Achievement Act was introduced in Congress in spring 2017 to appropriate grants to "assist early childhood education programs in carrying out early childhood STEM programs/activities," which can be used for professional development, materials and equipment, and establishing partnerships with institutions of higher education to provide training for preschool teachers.

Much more opportunity exists within the recently passed Every Student Succeeds Act (ESSA), which contains several possibilities for early STEM education, especially with a focus on engaging families. Although not explicitly stated within ESSA, STEM skills and competencies can be strengthened through regulations that are stipulated within the law including enhanced transitions from preschool to kindergarten, stronger alignment of standards, curricula, and assessments, and data sharing between teachers, school leaders, and parents. For instance, STEM activities could be integrated into transition planning, explicitly focused on in standards, and a particular point of conversations and data sharing. Additionally, the ESSA requires districts receiving Title I funds to submit a written parent and family engagement policy, focusing on establishing expectations for meaningful engagement. STEM could be a topic around which families and schools join together meaningfully to promote children's learning.

Early learning in general also received a significant amount of attention in the ESSA; focusing on addressing gaps in STEM skills early can hold several positive implications. Enhanced professional development can be provided that would include STEM education instructional training for preschool through third grade teachers and administrators, with a family engagement component. Enhanced reporting and accountability structures will require more transparency around resource and personnel allocations, which could potentially include STEM programming and curricula. Lastly, increased allowable funding for afterschool and enrichment STEM programs is included. These strategies allow states to set up strong platforms for successful family engagement and the development of early STEM skills and competencies.

RECOMMENDATIONS

To successfully engage parents in developing their children's early STEM skills, the following recommendations are offered:

- **Frame policy and public awareness campaigns around available research on the importance of early STEM learning.** Research clearly shows the importance of early STEM for children's educational and economic outcomes. Policymakers can use this research to frame messages that develop family and community awareness of the importance of early STEM. This recommendation also applies to state lawmakers, providing them with the data and dialogue for building political coalitions focused on early STEM education. Early childhood education researchers and advocates are key players in the implementation of this recommendation as well. Governors are also a critical group to focus on, as they have the capacity for funding and oversight of STEM advisory councils and other action-oriented groups.
- **Use public funds to pilot STEM and family engagement initiatives.** States and federal legislatures are taking the lead in developing new and innovative programs that promote high-quality STEM teaching and learning. These funds can be used to pilot different ways to engage families.
- **Empower parents to advocate for stronger STEM policies.** Policies can be put in place to educate and empower parents and families to become STEM advocates for their children, at both the school and policy levels.
- **Target outreach and programs to underserved communities.** Given the preponderance of research pointing to inequalities in opportunities for STEM learning, especially among low-income students, communities of color, and English language learners, initiatives can target these groups specifically.
- **Create an accessible, understandable online database of exemplary programs.** This database can include peer-reviewed research summaries, instructional lessons, and other resources for program developers, researchers, and parents. The database can also include informal surveys that program providers can use to systematically track long-term STEM education achievement and trends.

CONCLUSION

Parents and families are critical to the development of their children's early STEM skills; they need to become empowered and informed consumers of educational research, overcome personal and/or public assumptions and biases, and advocate for their children. The recommendations presented above are policy-level initiatives designed to help parents do so. These actions can help improve long-term STEM educational skills, especially for underserved populations. But parents and families need support in their efforts: early childhood STEM researchers and advocates must come up with a unified approach to pave the way. The Joan Ganz Cooney Center and the Erikson Institute have both developed publications to improve early STEM education that are both comprehensive and engaging (Bowman et al., 2017; McClure et al., 2017).

The recommendations here have the potential to strengthen the country's STEM workforce by providing a prepared, educated citizenry capable of fulfilling the many openings in STEM positions, and to reestablish the U.S. as a predominant global economic competitor and educational leader. The presented policies share several commonalities: they incorporate sustainable funding (whether direct or braided), allow for high quality programs, have accountability and continuous improvement mechanisms implicit, and have the oversight of STEM advisory councils, and legislative (and executive) champions behind them to move the work forward. Although several policy strategies and programs exist, the onus falls to families to provide the early foundational STEM skills and competencies children need to be successful. Policies and programs can then serve to compliment and strengthen these efforts once children formally enter the school system.

REFERENCES

ACT, Inc. (2017). *The condition of college and career readiness, 2016*. Retrieved from https://www.act.org/content/dam/act/unsecured/documents/CCCR_National_2016.pdf

Aikens, N., Atkins-Burnett, S., & Bandel, E. (2012). *Approaches to addressing the language and literacy skills of young dual language learners: A review of the research, Research Brief #10*. Chapel Hill, NC: University of North Carolina.

Amsterlaw, J., & Wellman, H. M. (2006). Theories of mind in transition: A microgenetic study of the development of false belief understanding. *Journal of Cognition and Development*, 7(2), 139–172. doi:10.1207/s15327647jcd0702_1

Bassok, D., & Latham, S. (2017). The rise in children's academic skills at kindergarten entry. *Educational Researcher*, 46(1), 1–14. doi:https://doiorg/10.3102/0013189X17694161

Bayer Corporation. (2015). *Bayer facts of science education XVII–2015*. Retrieved from http://www.msms.bayer.us/msms/MSMS_ Education_Resources_Activities/ResourcesSTP/Survey/Assets/Bayer_Facts_16_Exec_Summary2015.pdf

Belfali, Y., & Ikeda, M. (2016). *Country note: Key findings from PISA 2015 for the United States*. Paris, France: Organization for Economic and Co-operation and Development. Retrieved from http://www.oecd.org/pisa/pisa-2015-United-States.pdf

Bowman, B., Brunson-Day, C., Chen, J., Cunningham, C., Donohue, C., Espinosa, L., ... Worth, K. (2017, January). *Early STEM Matters: Providing high quality STEM experiences for all young learners.* Chicago, IL: University of Chicago STEM Education & Erikson Institute. Retrieved from https://50.erikson.edu/wp-content/uploads/2017/01/STEM-Working-Group-Report.pdf

Bureau of Labor Statistics. (2015, December 17). *Occupational outlook handbook: Computer and information technology occupations.* Retrieved from https://www.bls.gov/ooh/computer-and-information-technology/home.htm

Carnevale, A. P., Smith, N., Stone, J. R., Kotamraju, P., Steuernagel, B., & Green, K. A. (2011). *Career clusters: Forecasting demand for high school through career jobs, 2008–2018.* Washington, DC: Georgetown Center on Education and the Workforce. Retrieved from https://cew.georgetown.edu/wp-content/uploads/2014/11/clusters-complete-update1-1.pdf

Crowley, K., Callanan, M. A., Tenenbaum, H. R., & Allen, E. (2001). Parents explain more often to boys than to girls during shared scientific thinking. *Psychological Science, 12*(3), 258–261. doi:https://doi.org/10.1111/1467-9280.00347

Dodge, K. A., Bai, Y., Ladd, H. F., & Muschkin, C. G. (2016). Impact of North Carolina's early childhood programs and policies on educational outcomes in elementary school. *Child Development, 88*(3), 996–1014. doi:10.1111/cdev.12645

Duncan, G. J., Dowsett, C. J., Claessens, A., Magnuson, K., Huston, A. C., ... Japel, C. (2007). School readiness and later achievement. *Developmental Psychology, 43*(6), 1428–1446. doi:10.1037/0012-1649.43.6.1428

Goldenberg, C. (2008). Teaching English language learners: What the research does and does not say. *American Educator, Summer,* 8–44. Retrieved from https://www.aft.org/sites/default/files/periodicals/goldenberg.pdf

Gopnik, A., Meltzoff, A. N., & Kuhl, P. K. (2000). *The scientist in the crib: What early learning tells us about the mind.* New York: HarperCollins.

Gottfried, M. A., & Williams, D. N. (2013). STEM club participation and STEM schooling outcomes. *Education Policy Analysis Archives, 21*(79), 1–27. doi:http://dx.doi.org/10.14507/epaa.v21n79.2013. Retrieved from http://epaa.asu.edu/ojs/article/view/1361/1167

Huang, F. L. (2017). Does attending a state-funded preschool program improve letter name knowledge? *Early Childhood Research Quarterly, 38*(1), 116–126. doi:https://doi.org/10.1016/j.ecresq.2016.08.002

Jackson, R., & King, M. P. (2016). *Increasing students' access to opportunity in STEM by effectively engaging families.* Alexandria, VA: National Parent Teacher Association. Retrieved from https://s3.amazonaws.com/rdcms-pta/files/production/public/Images/STEM_Whitepaper_FINAL.pdf

Jordan, N. C., Kaplan, D., Oláh, L. N., & Locuniak, M. N. (2006). Number sense growth in kindergarten: A longitudinal investigation of children at risk for mathematics difficulties. *Child Development, 77*(1), 153–175. doi:10.1111/j.1467-8624.2006.00862.x

Langdon, D., McKittrick, G., Beede, D., Khan, B., & Doms, M. (2011, July). *STEM: Good jobs now and for the future* [ESA Issue Brief #03-11]. U.S. Department of Commerce, Economics and Statistics Administration. Retrieved from http://www.esa.doc.gov/sites/default/files/stemfinaljuly14_1.pdf

Levine, S. C., Suriyakham, L., Rowe, M. L., Huttenlocher, J., & Gunderson, E. A. (2010). What counts in the development of young children's number knowledge? *Developmental Psychology, 46*(5), 1309–1319. doi:10.1037/a0019671

Lipsey, M. W., Farran, D. C., & Hofer, K. G. (2015). *A randomized control trial of a statewide voluntary prekindergarten program on children's skills and behaviors through third grade* (Research Report). Nashville, TN: Vanderbilt University, Peabody Research Institute.

McClure, E. R., Guernsey, L., Clements, D. H., Bales, S. N., Nichols, J., Kendall-Taylor, N., & Levine, M. H. (2017). *STEM starts early: Grounding science, technology, engineering, and math education in early childhood.* New York, NY: The Joan Ganz Cooney Center at Sesame Workshop. Retrieved from https://na-production.s3.amazonaws.com/documents/jgcc_stemstartsearly_final.pdf

Morgan, P. L., Farkas, G., Hillemeier, M. M., & Maczuga, S. (2016). Science achievement gaps begin very early, persist, and are largely explained by modifiable factors. *Educational Researcher, 45*(1), 18–35. doi:https://doi.org/10.3102/0013189X16633182

National Assessment of Educational Progress. (2015). *The nation's report card-2015; 4th and 8th Grade mathematics assessments.* Retrieved from https://www.nationsreportcard.gov/reading_math_2015/#mathematics?grade=4

New American Economy (2017, March 29). *Sizing up the gap in our supply of STEM workers.* Retrieved from http://www.newamericaneconomy.org/research/sizing-up-the-gap-in-our-supply-of-stem-workers/

Organization for Economic Co-operation and Development (OECD). (2015). *The ABCs of gender equality in education: Aptitude, behavior, confidence.* Paris, France: Author. Retrieved from https://www.oecd.org/pisa/keyfindings/pisa-2012-results-gender-eng.pdf

Phillips, D., Gormley, W., & Anderson, S. (2016). The effects of Tulsa's CAP Head Start program on middle-school academic outcomes and progress. *Developmental Psychology, 52*(8), 1247–1261. doi:10.1037/dev0000151

Phillips, D., Lipsey, M. W., Dodge, K. A., Haskins, R., Bassok, D., … Weiland, C. (2017). *Puzzling it out: The current state of scientific knowledge on pre-kindergarten effects, a consensus statement.* Washington, DC: Brookings Institution. Retrieved from https://www.brookings.edu/wp-content/uploads/2017/04/duke_prekstudy_final_4-4-17_hires.pdf

Pruden, S. M., Levine, S. C., & Huttenlocher, J. (2011). Children's spatial thinking: Does talk about the spatial world matter? *Developmental Science, 14*(6), 1417–1430. doi:10.1111/j.1467-7687.2011.01088.x

Reardon, S. F., & Portilla, X. A. (2016). Recent trends in income, racial and ethnic school readiness gaps at kindergarten entry. *AERA Open, 2*(3), 1–18. doi:https://doi.org/10.1177/2332858416657343

Ruiz Soto, A. G., Hooker, S., & Batalova, J. (2015, June). States and districts with the highest number and share of English language learners. *Migration Policy Institute.* Retrieved from http://www.migrationpolicy.org/research/states-and-districts-highest-number-and-share-english-language-learners

Schleicher, A. (2016). *Program for International Student Assessment (PISA) 2015: PISA results in focus.* Paris, France: Organization for Economic Co-operation and

Development. Retrieved from http://www.oecd.org/pisa/pisa-2015-results-in-focus.pdf

Schleicher, A., & Davidson, M. (2013). *Program for International Student Assessment (PISA): Results from PISA 2012 (United States)*. Paris, France: Organization for Economic Co-operation and Development. Retrieved from http://www.oecd.org/unitedstates/PISA-2012-results-US.pdf

Stahl, A. E., & Feigenson, L. (2015). Observing the unexpected enhances infants' learning and exploration. *Science, 348*(6230), 91–94. doi:10.1126/science.aaa3799

Tytler, R., & Peterson, S. (2003). Tracing young children's scientific reasoning. *Research in Science Education, 33*(4), 433–465. doi:https://doi.org/10.1023/B:RISE.0000005250.04426.67

U.S. Department of Education, National Center for Education Statistics, Common Core of Data. (2016). *Local education agency universe survey, 2004–05 through 2014–15*. Retrieved from https://nces.ed.gov/programs/digest/d16/tables/dt16_204.20.asp

Watts, T. W., Duncan, G. J., Siegler, R. S., & Davis-Kean, P. E. (2014). What's past is prologue: Relations between early mathematics knowledge and high school achievement. *Educational Researcher, 43*(7), 352–360. doi:https://doi.org/10.3102/0013189X14553660

Woodward, A. L. (2009). Infants' grasp of others' intentions. *Current Directions in Psychological Science, 18*(1), 53–57. doi:10.1111/j.1467-8721.2009.01605.x

CHAPTER 11

HOW THE NATIONAL SCIENCE FOUNDATION SUPPORTS FAMILY ENGAGEMENT IN STEM LEARNING

Joan Walker

When researchers and educators who value family engagement think about support for their work, the National Science Foundation (NSF) may not be the first resource that comes to mind. This is unfortunate given that the agency offers a variety of funding opportunities and practitioner resources relevant to family engagement. This chapter is designed to inform readers about how NSF's Directorate of Education and Human Resources (EHR) funds research examining relations among families' home-, school- and community-based activities, student interest in science, technology, engineering, and mathematics (STEM) and the development of students' STEM knowledge over time. A second goal is to provide potential grant applicants with information about how to propose a family engagement project to NSF.

To achieve these goals, this chapter: (1) describes a sample of four EHR programs; (2) provides examples of work recently funded by each program; and (3) highlights publicly available resources that support family engagement practitioners and the development of research grant proposals. As

Promising Practices for Engaging Families in STEM Learning, pp. 161–171
Copyright © 2018 by Information Age Publishing
All rights of reproduction in any form reserved.

the examples and resources will show, NSF supports research involving a range of participants (e.g., children, parents, teachers), ecological spheres of development (e.g., home, school, community), and outcomes of interest (e.g., child achievement, family participation in school activities). Moreover, the examples illustrate the Foundation's goal of distributing federal dollars equitably across a range of STEM content areas, investigator career stages, and research participant demographics.

Advancements in our understanding of the essential role that families play in STEM learning can be summarized in three evidence-based themes. First, early experience matters. For example, science achievement gaps begin early, are durable, and can be explained by modifiable factors, including children's knowledge, child- and family-level characteristics (e.g., parenting quality), and school-level characteristics (Morgan, Farkas, Hillemeier & Maczuga, 2016). Second, families continue to make significant contributions to students' STEM learning and engagement across adolescence. For example, mothers' explanations about the usefulness of mathematics and science predicted adolescents' interest in and valuing of those STEM content areas, as well as their mathematics and science course-taking (Hyde et al., 2017). Finally, motivational supports, sometimes referred to as "academic socialization supports" (Hill & Tyson, 2009) or "subtle" forms of family engagement (Jeynes, 2010), such as expressing high educational aspirations and communicating with students about school, have greater impact on student achievement than more specific and supervisory "parents-helping-with-homework" behaviors that typically come to mind (Fan & Chen, 2001).

Evidence that families contribute to large variations in students' STEM knowledge and interest development points to the need for educational reform strategies that involve families. Specifically, the three evidence-based themes highlighted above underscore the need for programs and policies that: (1) promote simple, low-cost, and effective tools that families can use to prepare their children for educational success; and (2) support conditions that protect and facilitate families' motivation to use those tools.

Although the field of family engagement research has made important strides in the last 30 years, there is still much to learn about why families become involved, what they do when they are involved, and how their involvement translates into student outcomes. How can NSF help you to further transform our understanding of family engagement in STEM education? The next section addresses this question.

A SAMPLE OF PROGRAMS, FUNDED PROJECTS, AND PROGRAM RESOURCES

NSF's Division of Research on Learning in Formal and Informal Environments (DRL) offers several funding streams that support the exploration, design, and testing of pathways for family and student engagement in anywhere, anytime STEM learning. This section describes a sample of four programs that support basic and applied research. Table 11.1 summarizes each program's aims.

Table 11.1.
Description of Four Programs Supported by the Division of Research on Learning in Formal and Informal Environments

EHR Program	Description
EHR Core Research (ECR)	Seeks proposals that synthesize, build, and/or expand foundational/basic research in the following areas: STEM learning, STEM learning environments, STEM workforce development, and broadening participation in STEM.
Discovery Research PreK–12 (DRK-12)	Seeks to advance pre-K-12 student and teacher learning of the STEM disciplines, through research and development of innovative resources, models, and technologies for use by students, teachers, administrators, and policymakers.
Innovative Technology Experiences for Students and Teachers (ITEST)	Seeks to engage students, educators, and families in the creative use of information technologies within the context of STEM learning experiences in school and other learning settings. ITEST projects must include research on student outcomes.
Advancing Informal STEM Learning (AISL)	Builds on educational research and practice, and seeks to increase interest in, engagement with, and understanding of STEM by individuals of all ages and backgrounds through self-directed STEM learning experiences.

These four programs welcome any of the following three types of family engagement research: (1) studies to advance foundational knowledge that guides theory development; (2) Early-Stage or Exploratory research to identify evidence of the promise (or lack thereof) of programs, policies, or practices; and (3) Late-Stage Design and Development research that guides the development and early-stage testing of innovative programs, policies, and practices to improve education outcomes. Taken from the Common Guidelines developed by NSF and the Institute for Education Science, Table 11.2 summarizes the respective purposes and requirements of each type of research.

Table 11.2.
Descriptions of Foundational, Early-Stage or Exploratory, and Design and Development Studies

Foundational Research	Advances the frontiers of education and learning; develops and refines theory and methodology; and provides fundamental knowledge about teaching and/or learning. Foundational research studies may examine phenomena without establishing an explicit link to educational outcomes.
Early-Stage or Exploratory Research	Investigates approaches to education problems to establish the basis for design and development of new interventions or strategies, and/or to provide evidence for whether an established intervention or strategy is ready to be tested in an efficacy study. Research in this category should establish initial connections to outcomes of interest. Studies in this genre should support the development of a well-explicated theory of action that can inform the development, modification, or evaluation of an intervention or strategy.
Design and Development Research	Develops new or improved interventions or strategies to achieve well-specified learning goals or objectives, including making refinements based on small-scale testing. Typically, this research involves four components: (1) development of a solution based on a well-specified theory of action appropriate to a well-defined end user; (2) creation of measures to assess the implementation of the solution(s); (3) collection of data on the feasibility of implementing the solution(s) in typical delivery settings by intended users; and (4) conducting a pilot study to examine the promise of generating intended outcomes. In some cases, funders will expect all four stages to be completed within a single project; in other cases, design and development projects may entail sequential projects.

BASIC RESEARCH: THE EDUCATION AND HUMAN RESOURCE'S CORE RESEARCH (ECR) PROGRAM

How and why do families make a difference in students' STEM-related outcomes? This is the essential question undertaken by EHR's Core Research (ECR) program. It provides funding in critical research areas that are essential, broad, and enduring. The ECR program supports fundamental research on STEM learning and education by fostering efforts to develop foundational knowledge in STEM learning and learning contexts, both formal and informal. To increase public understanding of science and engineering, it funds research involving all age groups, from the earliest developmental stages of life through adulthood and participation in the workforce. It seeks proposals that will help synthesize, build and/or expand research foundations in the following focal areas: STEM learning, STEM learning environments, STEM workforce development, and broadening participation in STEM.

Example of ECR grants. *Developing Critical STEM Thinkers: Optimizing Explanations in Inquiry-Based Learning* led by Kathleen Corriveau (National Science Foundation, 2017a) pursues the fundamental question of how children acquire STEM knowledge from social resources. For example, in science learning it is often accepted that children learn best when they acquire information from first-hand experience. However, many times, both at home and at school, first-hand information is not available. In these cases, students rely on an explanation given to them by a caregiver or teacher. How adults choose to provide explanations can vary dramatically, and aspects of the explanation itself can shape children's future learning (Corriveau & Kurkul, 2014; Kurkul & Corriveau, 2017). Consistent with the need for simple, low-cost, and effective tools that help families prepare their young children for STEM educational success, this project examines how the quality of families' and teachers' explanations of scientific phenomena relate to children's understanding and exploratory behaviors in preschool classrooms and in children's science museums.

Specifically, the study is using: (1) observations of questions and explanations in adult-child interactions in an inquiry-based preschool; (2) systematic experiments in both laboratory and museum settings to explore how various aspects of an explanation impact children's learning; and (3) an intervention designed to promote scientific thinking between parents and children in a museum setting. Ultimately, this work can support families' and teachers' motivation to use questioning as a low-cost and readily available tool for supporting children's STEM learning. Integrated throughout the research are several educational activities designed to promote broader public awareness of the importance of social interaction to children's STEM learning. For example, this project creates partnerships with local museums, offers training and mentoring to graduate, undergraduate, and high school research students, and designs professional development workshops for museum educators. In addition to exemplifying ECR's program goals, this project is an example of the Foundation's CAREER program, which supports junior faculty who exemplify the next generation of teacher-scholars through outstanding research, excellent education, and the integration of education and research.

***

If we know how it works, then can we make it work more effectively? This is the essential question undertaken by DRL's applied programs, which focus on teaching and learning, assessment, and workforce development in formal and informal learning environments. Three applied programs, distinguishable by their ecological settings, are described in the following sections.

Formal Learning Environments: Discovery Research Pre-K–12 (DRK-12)

DRK-12 seeks to significantly enhance the learning and teaching of STEM by pre-K–12 students and teachers, through research and development of STEM education innovations and approaches. The DRK-12 program has three major research and development strands: (1) assessment, (2) learning, and (3) teaching.

Example of a DRK-12 grant. *A Research-Practice Collaboration to Improve Math Learning in Young Children* led by Susan Levine (National Science Foundation, 2015a) brings together a diverse group of experts to: (1) examine how mathematical knowledge and attitudes together affect early mathematical achievement; and (2) develop tools that promote learning at home and in school for children from kindergarten to grade three. Success in mathematics requires learning content, but also has social and emotional dimensions. Yet mathematical instruction does not typically address the emotional dimension. This is problematic because many parents and elementary school teachers have both high levels of math anxiety and less-than-optimal knowledge of how to promote mathematical learning and interest in young children. The result is a cycle of intergenerational transmission of low mathematical achievement and high math anxiety (Maloney, Ramirez, Gunderson, Levine, & Beilock, 2015).

To break this cycle, the network is bringing together: (1) researchers who study the knowledge and attitudes that support mathematical achievement; (2) developers who translate research findings into effective educational tools; (3) practitioners who implement educational tools in real-world learning settings; and (4) experts in the dissemination of such tools. By combining these different kinds of expertise, and by consulting with families, the network will develop and share a toolkit for parents and teachers to help them more effectively provide mathematical instruction to children from diverse socioeconomic backgrounds. This project is consistent with evidence that motivational or academic socialization supports are an important factor in student achievement. It also relates to the need for programs and policies that: (1) promote simple, low-cost, and effective tools that families can use to prepare their children for educational success; and (2) support conditions that protect and facilitate families' motivation to use those tools.

The 21st Century Workplace: Technology Experiences for Students and Teachers (ITEST)

ITEST is a program that promotes pre-K–12 student interests and capacities to participate in the STEM and information and communications technology (ICT) workforce of the future. It supports the development, implementation, and selective spread of innovative strategies for engaging students in experiences that: (1) increase awareness of STEM and ICT careers; (2) motivate students to pursue the education necessary to participate in those careers; and/or (3) provide students with technology-rich experiences that develop their knowledge of the content and skills needed for entering the STEM workforce. The ITEST program is especially interested in broadening participation of students from traditionally underrepresented groups in STEM fields and related education and workforce domains. Projects that actively engage business and industry partners to better ensure that pre-K-12 experiences foster the knowledge and skill-sets needed for emerging STEM-related occupations are strongly encouraged.

Example of an ITEST grant. *Project BUILD (Building Using an Interactive Learning Design)* led by Paul Dusenbery (National Science Foundation, 2017b) seeks to better understand and promote practices that increase students' motivation and capacity to pursue STEM careers. It brings together youth (grades 2 through 5), their families, librarians, and professional engineers across six different communities (three urban, three rural) in informal learning environments centered on engaging youth with age-appropriate, technology-rich STEM learning experiences fundamental to the engineering design process. The overarching aim is to better understand how youths' learning preferences or dispositions develop in relation to their STEM learning experiences. It also seeks to build community members' capacity to inspire and educate youth about STEM careers. Project BUILD extends the scope and reach of a prior NSF-funded project called the STAR Library Education Network (STAR_Net), which increased librarians and library staff's knowledge, interest, and confidence in offering STEM programming to their patrons. In turn, the libraries' STEM exhibits motivated many patrons to learn more about science and engineering (Fitzhugh & Coulon, 2015).

This project is another example of efforts to: (1) promote simple, low-cost, and effective tools that families can use to prepare their children for educational success; and (2) support conditions that protect and facilitate families' motivation to use those tools. It also speaks to evidence that motivational supports are critical to students' STEM achievement.

Out-of-School Learning Environments: Advancing Informal STEM Learning (AISL)

This program seeks to: (1) advance new approaches to and evidence-based understanding of the design and development of STEM learning opportunities for the public in informal environments; (2) provide multiple pathways for broadening access to and engagement in STEM learning experiences; and (3) advance innovative research on and assessment of STEM learning in informal settings.

Example of AISL grant. *The Latina SciGirls: Promoting Middle School-Age Hispanic Girls' Positive STEM Identity Development* project led by Rita Karl (National Science Foundation, 2015b) promotes positive STEM identity development in middle school-age Latina girls. Latina girls have high interest in STEM, high confidence, and a strong work ethic, but have less support and exposure to STEM professionals than their non-Latina White peers (Modi, Schoenberg, & Salmond, 2012). In cooperation with Twin Cities Public Television (TPT), the project is addressing this gap by producing *Latina SciGirls*, a fourth season of the Emmy Award-winning television and transmedia project *SciGirls*, which demonstrated that incorporating multimedia is an effective method for influencing girls' interest, self-efficacy, and learning through citizen science (Flagg, 2016).

To engage both Latino parents and their daughters, TPT is creating a series of family- and girl-friendly online role model video profiles, in Spanish and English, of Latina STEM professionals. Further, the project provides opportunities to connect girls and their families with in-person Latina role models and STEM programming via community outreach in diverse Latino communities across the country. The *Latina SciGirls* television program includes six half-hour episodes filmed in Spanish, showing groups of Latinas and their Latina STEM mentors investigating culturally relevant science and engineering problems.

Episodes go beyond STEM "factoids" to highlight the process of science and engineering. Girls can see how choosing, questioning, planning, predicting, observing, interpreting, and communicating actually take place. They learn how rewarding and fun it is to do science and engineering with peers, and the show's female mentors offer girls a glimpse of exciting STEM career possibilities. In 2011, *SciGirls* won the Emmy Award for New Approaches, recognizing its innovative merging of TV and the web. *SciGirls* episodes have been broadcast over 72,640 times on 492 public television channels. The show is now featured on 92% of U.S. TV households. This project is an excellent example of research focused on developing a range of integrated social and motivational supports that families and others can use to foster underrepresented youths' participation in STEM.

RECOMMENDATIONS

The chapter concludes with three basic recommendations.

Recommendation 1: Learn More About NSF Programs and Previously Funded Projects

Visit each program's page on the NSF site. Each program's home page offers a link to recently funded projects. You can also watch brief videos describing NSF-funded education research projects at NSF's *STEM for All* video showcase.[1] These sites allow visitors to comment on projects, engage with project staff, and participate in facilitated conversations about the projects. You can also visit NSF's resource centers, including ITEST's STEM Learning and Research Center (STELAR, stelar.edc.org), AISL's Center for the Advancement of Informal Science Education (CAISE, informalscience. org), and DRK-12's Community for Advancing Discovery Research in Education (CADRE, cadrek12.org).

Keep in mind the NSF's goal is to invest public funding equitably. New investigators are encouraged to submit proposals. If you are unsure of how to apply, the foundation regularly holds webinars and conducts outreach. Contact your institution's development staff or office of sponsored research to learn more about these opportunities. And, don't be shy about contacting NSF directly. We serve the public interest and YOU are the public. Be strategic in contacting program officers; each program solicitation identifies cognizant program officers. An efficient approach is to prepare a one-page summary of your project's aims and e-mail it to a program officer attached to the program(s) that you think best fits your work. You can also access information about the proposal review process by entering "NSF merit review" into an online search. The merit review page also explains how you can become a reviewer, which is a great way to learn more about program requirements.

Recommendation 2: Look to Other Public Sources for Funding to Support Family Engagement and STEM

While NSF is an important promoter of family engagement and STEM, other federal agencies also provide support and opportunities in this area. For example, the Every Student Succeeds Act (ESSA) administered by the U.S. Department of Education requires that districts with Title 1 funds reserve at least 1% of those funds to carry out parent and family engagement activities. Districts can consider using Title I funds towards family engagement and STEM activities. The 21st Century Community Learning Centers program, also run by the U.S. Department of Education, provides federal funding to support out-of-school programs. The program has a strong commitment to STEM and family engagement can be incorporated here, too. Further, the Institute of Museum and Library Sciences provides grants to libraries and museums that focus on STEM learning, many of which can infuse family engagement into their offerings.

Recommendation 3: Consider Research-Practice Partnerships That Contribute to the Field and Help Improve Your Own Program

Many of the programs described in this chapter represent partnerships between university- or community-based researchers and education practitioners. As coequal partners, these teams explore innovations in family engagement and STEM education. Partnerships provide programs with opportunities to contribute to basic research, evaluation of promising program models, the piloting and developing of new ideas, and scaling up models that have demonstrated effectiveness. Partnerships can also help program developers plan and refine their own efforts.

NOTE

1. Access the video showcase at: http://stemforall2016.videohall.com/ and at http://stemforall2017.videohall.com/

REFERENCES

Corriveau, K. H., & Kurkul, K. E. (2014). "Why does rain fall?": Children prefer to learn from an informant who uses noncircular explanations. *Child Development, 85*(5), 1827–1835. doi:10.1111/cdev.12240

Kurkul, K. E., & Corriveau, K. H. (2017). Question, explanation, follow-up: A mechanism for learning from others? *Child Development. 89(1),* 280–294. doi:10.1111/cdev.12726

Fan, X., & Chen, M. (2001). Parental involvement and students' academic achievement: A meta-analysis. *Educational Psychology Review, 13*(1), 1–22. doi:https://doi.org/10.1023/A:1009048817385

Flagg, B. N. (2016). Contribution of multimedia to girls' experience of citizen science. *Citizen Science: Theory and Practice, 1*(2), 1–11. doi:10.5334/cstp.51

Fitzhugh G., & Coulon V. (2015). *Can libraries provide STEM learning experiences for patrons? Findings from the STAR_Net Project summative evaluation.* Paper presented at the Public Libraries & STEM Conference. Retrieved from http://www.starnetlibraries.org/stem-in-libraries/evaluation/

Hill, N. E., & Tyson, D. F. (2009). Parental involvement in middle school: A meta-analytic assessment of the strategies that promote achievement. *Developmental Psychology*, *45*(3), 740–763. doi:10.1037/a0015362

Hyde, J. S., Canning, E. A., Rozek, C. S., Clarke, E., Hulleman, C. S., & Harackiewicz, J. M. (2017). The role of mothers' communication in promoting motivation for math and science course-taking in high school. *Journal of Research on Adolescence*, *27*(1), 49–64. doi:10.1111/jora.12253

Jeynes, W. H. (2010). The salience of the subtle aspects of parental involvement and encouraging that involvement: Implications for school-based programs. *Teachers College Record*, *112*(3), 747–774.

Maloney, E. A., Ramirez, G., Gunderson, E. A., Levine, S. C., & Beilock, S. L. (2015). Intergenerational effects of parents' math anxiety on children's math achievement and anxiety. *Psychological Science*, *26*(9), 1480–1488. doi:10.1177/0956797615592630

Modi, K., Schoenberg, J., & Salmond, K. (2012). *Generation STEM: What girls say about science, technology, engineering, and math.* New York, NY: Girl Scouts of the USA.

Morgan, P. L., Farkas, G., Hillemeier, M. M., & Maczuga, S. (2016). Science achievement gaps begin very early, persist, and are largely explained by modifiable factors. *Educational Researcher*, *45*(1), 18–35. doi:10.3102/0013189X16633182

National Science Foundation. (2015a). *SL–CN: A research-practice collaboration to improve math learning in young children.* Retrieved from https://www.nsf.gov/awardsearch/showAward?AWD_ID=1540741

National Science Foundation. (2015b). *Latina SciGirls: Promoting middle school-age Hispanic girls' positive STEM identity development.* Retrieved from https://www.nsf.gov/awardsearch/showAward?AWD_ID=1515507

National Science Foundation. (2017a). *CAREER: Developing critical STEM thinkers: Optimizing explanations in inquiry-based learning.* Retrieved from https://www.nsf.gov/awardsearch/showAward?AWD_ID=1652224&HistoricalAwards=false

National Science Foundation. (2017b). *Project BUILD (building using an interactive learning design).* Retrieved from https://www.nsf.gov/awardsearch/showAward?AWD_ID=1657593&HistoricalAwards=false

ABOUT THE AUTHORS

THE EDITORS

Margaret Caspe, is the director of research and professional learning at Global Family Research Project. She has over 15 years of experience working with schools, early childhood programs, libraries, research and evaluation organizations, and foundations to promote family engagement in children's learning. Prior to this position, Margaret worked with Harvard Family Research Project where among other efforts she co-led the *Libraries for the 21st Century: It's a Family Thing* initiative and developed resources for the Office of Head Start National Center for Parent, Family, and Community Engagement. She is coeditor of *Promising Practices for Engaging Families in Literacy* (IAP) and author of a variety of reports and articles. Margaret received her PhD in Applied Psychology from The Steinhardt School of Culture, Education, and Human Development at New York University and she holds an EdM from the Harvard Graduate School of Education. She is based in New Jersey where she and her three daughters count going to makerspaces among their favorite family activities.

Taniesha A. Woods, is an independent consultant. Throughout Woods's career she has worked at the intersection of research and policy where a recurring theme is the study of issues related to educational equity. Woods believes a focus on early mathematics education is critical to all children getting off to a strong start in school and life. Much of her published work has focused on early mathematics education, teacher professional development, and racial identity development. Currently, Taniesha is an independent consultant and her work focuses data analytics, research, and related policy that pertain to early care and education and children and families. Previously, Woods was the Director of Child Care Data Analytics at the NYC Department of Health and Mental Hygiene's (DOHMH) Bureau of Environmental Surveillance and Policy where she conducted data analysis on the quality of child care programs and homes throughout the five boroughs. Early in her career, Taniesha served as a Congressional fellow through the Society for Research in Child Development /American Association for the Advancement of Science on the U.S. Health, Education, Labor, and Pensions Committee where her portfolio included K–12 and higher education issues. Dr. Woods hold a PhD in developmental psychology with a formal concentration in quantitative psychology from the University of North Carolina at Chapel Hill and a BA in psychology and African and African American Studies from the University of Oklahoma. In her spare time, she enjoys arts/cultural and outdoor activities with her husband.

Joy Lorenzo Kennedy, is a developmental psychologist, and the scientific support specialist for Databrary, a web-based platform for sharing developmental research. Dr. Kennedy's research focuses on language and literacy development in early childhood, including program evaluation and improving family engagement. Dr. Kennedy's recent work has focused on improving access—access to programs by low-income parents, and access to data for behavioral researchers. She is coinvestigator on an R03 grant testing the impact of programmatic tweaks informed by behavioral economics on new mothers' use of existing language and literacy programs in New York City. The project aims to demonstrate that small, low-cost modifications can improve mothers' uptake of program recommendations, giving them better access to resources that will benefit their infants' growth and development. At Databrary, Dr. Kennedy promotes the sharing and reuse of research data, providing behavioral scientists—including students, early career researchers, and those from institutions with limited funding—equal access to a wide range of data for secondary analysis. Dr. Kennedy received her undergraduate degree in Psychology from Brown University, and her doctorate from the Developmental Psychology program in Applied Psychology at New York University.

THE AUTHORS

Ma. Victoria Almeda is a doctoral research fellow at Teachers College, Columbia University.

Oscar A. Barbarin is professor and chair of the African American Studies Department, University of Maryland, College Park.

Sian L. Beilock is president of Barnard College, Columbia University.

Talia Berkowitz is a doctoral student in The Department of Psychology, The University of Chicago.

Kimberly Brenneman is a program officer in education at the Heising-Simons Foundation.

Jeffrey Brown is an assistant professor in the Psychology Department at Minnesota State University, Mankato.

Maureen Callanan is a professor in the Psychology Department at University of California, Santa Cruz.

Margaret Caspe is director of research and professional learning at Global Family Research Project.

Tara Chklovski is founder and CEO of Iridescent.

Helena Duch wrote her chapter when she worked as an assistant professor at Columbia University Mailman School of Public Health. She is now a program officer for the Oak Foundation.

Lisa A. Gennetian is a research professor at The Institute for Human Development and Social Change, Steinhardt School of Culture, Education, and Human Development, New York University.

Herbert Ginsburg is the Jacob H. Schiff Foundation Professor of Psychology and Education Emeritus at Teachers College, Columbia University.

Daryl Greenfield is a professor of psychology & pediatrics at University of Miami.

Andrés Henríquez is vice president of STEM learning in communities at the New York Hall of Science.

Maggie Jaris is communications manager of Iridescent.

M. Elena Lopez is co-director of Global Family Research Project.

Susan C. Levine is the Rebecca Anne Boylan Professor in Education and Society in The Department of Psychology, The University of Chicago.

Christine M. McWayne is a professor and director of early childhood education at Eliot-Pearson Department of Child Study and Human Development at Tufts University.

Jayanthi Mistry is a professor at Eliot-Pearson Department of Child Study and Human Development at Tufts University.

Christopher S. Rozek is a postdoctoral scholar in The Department of Psychology, The University of Chicago.

Marjorie W. Schaeffer is a doctoral student in The Department of Psychology, The University of Chicago.

Cassandra Schreiber is a doctoral candidate in the Psychology Department at Minnesota State University, Mankato.

Graciela Solis is a postdoctoral scholar in the Psychology Department at Loyola University, Chicago.

Colleen Uscianowski is a doctoral research fellow at Teachers College, Columbia University.

Joan Walker is an associate professor in the School of Education at Pace University.

Matthew Weyer is a senior policy specialist at the National Conference of State Legislatures.

Betty Zan is an associate professor in the Department of Curriculum and Instruction at University of Northern Iowa.